WHERE THE WASHINGTONIANS
LIVED

Where the WASHINGTONIANS LIVED

* INTERESTING EARLY HOMES AND THE *
PEOPLE WHO BUILT AND LIVED IN THEM.

Photographs by Werner
LENGGENHAGER

Text by Lucile
McDONALD

SUPERIOR PUBLISHING COMPANY - SEATTLE

CONTENTS

Here's an odd fragment of decoration on an empty house at West 2010 Second Avenue, Spokane. Its present owner said artists are always finding it interesting to sketch. As the property has been for sale, probably this true gingerbread relic is doomed soon to disappear.

Preface

The search for Washington's picturesque houses has carried us through a cross section of the population, from the early settler with his Indian wife to the millionaire industrialist, from farmer to governor, from seaman to judge.

Today more is being done to rescue log cabins from decay than to save the Victorian houses. Pioneer cabins are in demand for removal to parks and several towns have used them as a nucleus for a village complex. Others have housed museum collections.

The average Victorian cottage, usually centrally located, has been a victim of freeways and new construction. A different fate has been dealt the spacious homes of yesterday's tycoons—the mansions have been divided into apartments or converted into dormitories or quarters for group enterprises. It is a rare house of this type that has survived as a single residence unit.

In the preparation of this book it was impossible to photograph every dwelling that deserved to be included. In a few instances the present-day owners objected, in others information was lacking or the premises were too decrepit. Then there were the sheer limitations of a volume this size. Purposely we have omitted most of the types of houses of the last 50 years and have endeavored to give readers an appreciation of home concepts of the earlier period and knowledge of where to look for examples.

Credit for this book belongs in part to the many librarians, members of historical and patriotic societies and other amiable persons who have assisted us in locating these houses and learning their history.

PUBLISHER'S NOTE: Problems of make-up and layout have not always permitted the text to be adjacent to the picture to which it refers, but description and photograph are in the same sequence. We earnestly hope that the reader, understanding this, will have no difficulty in relating text to picture.

White men found the Indians living simply. In 1841 artists with the United States Exploring Expedition sketched these types of abode:

WICKIUPS made of tule mats for summer camps.

SKIN TEPEES used by tribes east of the Cascades.

FISHING HUTS near the rapids of the Columbia. They had slightly sunken earth floors and walls assembled of mats and driftwood.

IN THE BEGINNING

Scientists search in the earth for signs of ancient habitations that tell the story of mankind and how he once lived. In a comparatively new land like the Pacific Northwest it was but a short step from the cedar-plank longhouse of the coastal tribes, the rock shelter or the skin-roofed pit dwelling of the interior Indians to the log cabin of the pioneer. The invading white man spread over the country quickly, bringing new ways that superseded those of the aboriginal people. Pit houses and cave dwellings were abandoned very early in the historic period. The tepee and tule-mat hut, employed in summer encampments, went out within a few years. With the moving of Indians to reservations the plank houses gradually ceased to serve and frame shanties took their place.

There are few remains of original Indian dwellings and one must turn to museums to learn of the native mode of life. But it is different with the white man; the story of his habits and habitations survives in his buildings, if you know where to find them.

In a land filled with trees, wooden structures were to be expected. Wood was a building material so cheap it was expendable. A quick shelter could be fashioned from logs with the help of stalwart sons or neighbors.

Sawmills began operation so early that soon it was not necessary to build homes much different from those to which the settlers were accustomed. It has been said that the forms these houses took were an indication of the owners' place of origin. Many were attractive and well proportioned, with clean, uncluttered lines. Later fashions in wood strayed from the severe, neatly mitred moldings to fretwork trims, fancy-cut shingles, Gothic towers, scrolls, brackets and bay windows.

We have attempted to recapture something of the past in this pictorial review of structures that reveal Washingtonians' practical customs and tastes, their foibles and fancies in the first century of white occupation.

ON THE STRAIT OF JUAN DE FUCA in 1857 Lieutenant Alden of the Coast Survey sketched Classet village near Cape Flattery, probably at present Warm Beach on the Makah Reservation.

PLANKS WERE USED in Indian houses on the edge of Port Townsend as late as the 1870's, when Harrison Eastman, San Francisco artist, made this drawing.

The first structures built for white men in Washington state were intended as the beginning of a Spanish settlement at Neah Bay in 1792. The artist, Josef Cordero, pictured them in the background of a sketch he made of Spanish and Indian craft in the harbor. No description of the buildings exists. They stood on a triangular piece of level ground just west of Village Creek. Evidently they were of poles set upright in the manner of tropical native villages constructed on the Mexican coast. The sharp peaked roofs were thatched with marsh grass.

Salvador Fidalgo, who commanded the Spanish expedition, reported he had erected a shed and a house with an oven for a bakery. He constructed corrals and a fortification with six mounted guns. He also planted a vegetable garden.

When the Indians killed one of Fidalgo's officers and he fired on a canoeload of the natives as punishment, relations with them became strained and the Spaniard was thankful to receive orders to leave.

Seven months after his expedition began the improvements it abandoned the port, then called Nunez Gaona, and never returned. After the Spaniards' departure the Indians, by their own account, threw bricks from the buildings into the brook and planted potatoes where the houses had stood. In a short time almost all traces of Spain's effort to colonize Washington were obliterated.

Sixty years later a New Englander, George O. Wilson, visited the site in a brig and told of finding a ruined stockade, which he mistakenly attributed to French builders.

Wilson related that while the brig was windbound in the bay Flattery Jack, the chief, invited the passengers ashore on a Sunday morning. "He escorted us to his house, which is about 50 feet long and 30 wide, made of boards hewn from trees," Wilson wrote. "A part of the tribe live in the house near him, the whole of which is enclosed by a strong barricade, said to be the remains of an old fort built by the French (Spanish) in former times."

This is the last mention of the old Spanish site by eyewitnesses. In another decade the place was overgrown with brush, the timbers were gone and only by diligent search were a few bricks (presumably from the bake oven) uncovered to indicate where the structures stood.

These Indian dwellings stand today on the old Spanish site at Neah Bay. They are part of the Makah Reservation.

Views A and B are from the harbor and show the true proportions of the hill behind the place where the Spaniards built.

View C is at the bridge over Village Creek, looking toward the same house as in View A, but from the side.

White men returned to Washington in the fur-trade period, living at first aboard their ships and seldom staying longer than a winter.

After the Astor post was founded on the Oregon side of the mouth of the Columbia River, the tendency was for any settlers to keep to the south of the stream until in 1824 Dr. John McLoughlin moved the Hudson's Bay Co. headquarters to Fort Vancouver. It became the greatest trading post west of the Mississippi, north of Monterery, Calif. and south of Sitka, Alaska. Dr. McLoughlin lived like a feudal overlord inside his stockade. Only "gentlemen" were housed within the stout fir-post enclosure. Outside dwelt the French Canadian company employes, some of whose abodes are shown in this sketch, made in 1845 by Lieut. Henry J. Warre, a British officer sent to survey fortifications. Some other artist must have added the feathers on the Indians, for those of the Columbia wore none.

A characteristic of the Hudson's Bay cabins was their mortised corners and solid, finished construction.

The stockade and company buildings were destroyed after 1853, American soldiers having been ordered to burn the walls. At the height of Fort Vancouver's prestige about 900 persons lived in and around it.

Relics of the early period are preserved in a National Parks Service museum adjacent to the original site, which is east of down-town Vancouver.

A survivor of the fur-trade period is the Covington house, located on Main Street (old U.S. 99) in Vancouver, north of West 39th Street. It is maintained as a public museum, open afternoons Tuesday through Sunday.

The home dates from 1848 and was built for Mr. and Mrs. Richard Covington, who arrived from London two years earlier to teach the school at Fort Vancouver. They took a land claim on April 11, 1848 at Fourth Plain, near present Orchards, and built the house at once. Covington was among the first to settle well in from the river.

The couple decided to quit the fort and establish a boarding school in the house. Census statistics show they had eight pupils in 1850 between the ages of 8 and 12. In another ten years the school had been discontinued and in 1867 the Covingtons sold the farm and moved to Washington, D.C.

Among the souvenirs they left behind was the first piano in the Pacific Northwest, which they had brought around Cape Horn. It was a Pleyel, from a famous manufacturer in Paris, and is now in the Fort Vancouver Historical Society Museum.

The Covington house was disassembled in 1928 and moved to city property. The Women's Club leased and maintained it.

As the Hudson's Bay Co. required a post midway between those on the Columbia and the Fraser Rivers, it founded Fort Nisqually in 1832. This is the way an artist and surveyor, Lieut. James Alden, saw it in 1857. The stockade was at present Dupont, close to the powder company gates. The site is well marked, so that a visitor still may find the location on a prairie.

Earlier than the fort here shown was another trading post on a bluff overlooking Puget Sound, just south of Sequalatchew Creek. Dr. William F. Tolmie, the factor, found the location not as good as that on the prairie, so he moved his headquarters and enclosed the new buildings in a stockade. The establishment gradually shifted its role from a fur-trading station to a large farm producing beef, hides, butter and cheese, which were shipped to Sitka and Hawaii, as well as to other company posts. It also shipped cedar shingles for use in California gold camps.

The United States took over the British holdings in 1867 and the buildings fell into ruins. What remained was moved to Point Defiance Park in Tacoma and reconstructed, using as much of the old materials as possible.

Among the structures moved from the Fort Nisqually site to Point Defiance Park was one which still stood in its original condition. Erected in 1843, it is the oldest white man's building in the state.

The little house, known as the granary because grain often was stored there, is characterized by an arched doorway and mortised corners. Its construction of square logs is typical of Hudson's Bay Co. carpentry.

During the Indian War company shepherds moved inside the stockade at Fort Nisqually for safety and took up residence in all available shelters. William Young, a Scotsman, and his wife Jane occupied the granary and there, on March 12, 1856, their first child, Janet Young, was born.

The factor's house is another of the Fort Nisqually buildings restored mostly of old material. Where timber had to be replaced it was done with new logs and planks whipsawed by hand and put together with hand-made oak pegs and nails.

The house was erected in 1857 while Dr. Tolmie still was factor. He was a University of Glasgow graduate and had studied medicine in Paris. Choice of him to head Fort Nisqually was accidental. He was on his way to supervise medical needs at other Hudson's Bay posts when a valued employe at Nisqually cut his foot badly, endangering his life. He was still in serious condition when the company bark on which Dr. Tolmie was traveling was ready to sail. The physician's baggage was put ashore in order that he might continue to attend the man.

Dr. Tolmie remained at Fort Nisqually most of the time until he was made a member of the company's board of management at Fort Victoria in 1859. He was succeeded by his chief clerk, Edward Huggins, who stayed on at Nisqually the rest of his

life and was the only other factor there after Dr. Tolmie.

The factor's house was one of the first frame structures built in Washington. It has a piazza, French windows and a fireplace in every room.

Before Fort Colville was established Father Pierre-Jean DeSmet, Jesuit missionary, visited the Indians gathered at Kettle Falls to fish. As many as 800 tribesmen might be there when the salmon were running.

Father DeSmet erected a temporary chapel of boughs on a high point and conducted services. The men were too busy spearing fish to attend, but the women and children flocked to the primitive church.

Although St. Paul's Mission was established in 1833 it was another five years before it had a more permanent structure. This in turn was replaced by

the building shown in the picture, said to have been erected in September, 1845 by Father Ravalli, assisted by the Indians. It was located half a mile from the fort.

The building was used until 1869, when St. Francis Regis Mission was founded north of the present town of Colville. St. Paul's was in a state of decay when the Washington State Parks and Recreation Commission made a project of restoring it, salvaging much of the original material. While other sites around Fort Colville were inundated by the waters of Lake Roosevelt after construction of Grand Coulee Dam, the mission remained out of reach of the Columbia. The surroundings look much as they did when the Indians thronged there long ago to worship.

West of the town of Ahtanum, at Parker, in Yakima County is a privately owned park with picnic facilities, for which a modest fee is charged. It contains four buildings, one of them the log church founded

in October, 1847. The structure is not the original built by Father Jean Charles Pandosy, Oblate of Mary Immaculate, which was burned in 1856 by Oregon Volunteers on an expedition against the Yakima Indians. Father Pandosy was ordered to abandon the station in March, 1859.

Eight years later Father Louis Napoleon St. Onge rebuilt the mission (page 16). It is a good example of mortise-and-tenon construction with squared logs.

In the days of the Oblates the building was both the residence of the priest and a church. Attached to it were a horse corral and enclosed garden. School was held in the building and furnishings were home-made tables and chairs. Heat was provided with a mud fireplace.

It is said that the first irrigation in Washington began at this place in 1852.

The early mission was destroyed after soldiers under Major J. G. Rains found a keg of powder buried in the garden. They supposed that the missionaries sympathized with the Indians and so burned the place.

The survivors reached Fort Vancouver September 22 to find it a hamlet consisting of about a dozen log cabins outside the Hudson's Bay Co. stockade and the small American garrison.

The only furniture that could be obtained was either home-made or secured from persons who had brought the pieces across the plains. The easy chair which Capt. Henry D. Wallin fashioned from a barrel and upholstered with calico stuffed with moss was the envy of his companions.

That winter was rainy and dismal and by spring the military colony hungered for garden produce. Some planted vegetables, but Captains Grant and Wallin borrowed money from Commander Bonneville, leased land and sowed barley, oats, onions, corn and potatoes.

After more buildings were erected to house the troops bachelor officers were assigned the so-called Grant mansion. Still later it became the officers' club at the fort. It is now a museum. Grant's bed, candle, foot locker and wardrobe are displayed there.

If one goes to the rear of the house he can see where the weatherboard siding has been removed, so that the old-type construction is visible.

In its first phase the upper story was used as living quarters for the commanding officer and staff. The lower floor was devoted to headquarters, the kitchen and the officers' mess. All construction work was by soldiers who received $1 a day extra duty pay.

Off the beaten track is the Columbia Lancaster house two miles north of Ridgefield, home of Washington Territory's first Delegate to Congress. Judge Lancaster was born at New Milford, Conn. in 1803, spent his youth in Ohio and studied law, practiced in Michigan and served as a member of the state legislature. In 1836 he went to Ohio to marry Rosannah Jones, by whom he had three children.

In 1842 the family left for Oregon, but as one daughter died and the wife became ill, they turned back and made a second start later in the year. Lancaster became chief justice of the provisional Supreme Court of Oregon Territory two months after their arrival. He ran for Delegate to Congress from Oregon in 1849 and was defeated. He received his patent for a donation land claim of 640 acres on the Lewis River and in 1851 represented the counties north of the Columbia in the Territorial Council. When Washington Territory was formed two years later he was chosen to represent it in Congress.

The Lancasters lived on the Ridgefield property until failing health forced them to sell and retire to Vancouver, where the judge died in 1893.

A description of the farm two years after his demise states that old Hudson's Bay Co. fur trails leading to it were still visible. The house was built after Lancaster's return from the congressional session and at that time was the finest residence in all of Washington Territory. The large pillared porches

were an idea the owner brought home from the national capital.

"On the floor of the parlor," the account related, is a finely preserved carpet of the oldest fashion. It is double-width Brussels, with patterns in red fully six feet long. The carpet was brought as a wedding present for Mrs. Lancaster and imported from London. The furniture, or most of it, is of mahogany with hair cloth seats and extremely quaint in design. All this furniture and carpet were brought across the plains by ox teams in 1849 and is all good for 50 years or more service."

In the attic were piled great stacks of books and public documents accumulated by the judge. Some bundles had been franked to him by the government for distribution to his constituents. Edmond S. Meany, the historian, undertook to rescue this material and carried it to Seattle for his library.

The present owner of the house, Aubrey Morgan, calls it by the Welsh name of Plas Newydd. The home was relocated to higher ground when the railroad was built nearby. The wing at the rear is a recent addition.

A landmark on old Highway 99 at Mary's Corner, south of Chehalis, is the log house erected by John R. Jackson in November, 1850. Long cared for by local clubs, it was taken over by the State Parks and Recreation Commission and preserved as a historic site. It was the home of the first American citizen (English-born, but naturalized) to take up land on the Cowlitz trail. It was Lewis County's first federal courthouse and served several times as the seat of county government. When county court was held here on November 12, 1850 the house was just finished.

One of Jackson's stepsons was laying shingles on the roof earlier that month when Judge William Strong rode by and called out, "Hurry up with that roof. I need your place for my courthouse."

The central portion of the dwelling, 16 by 26 feet in dimensions, was erected by Jackson and the boys in a week's time. It lacked puncheon floor and chimney and there were only openings for windows and doors when court opened.

Jackson had settled on the Cowlitz trail in 1845 in a small bachelor cabin. Three years later he married

Mrs. Matilda Koontz, a widow, and took her and her children from Oregon City to share his primitive home. When his bride first saw it the split-cedar door was fastened with wooden pegs and the chimney was made of sticks plastered inside with mud.

Better and more spacious quarters were needed. Travel was increasing on the trail and as soon as the new house was ready for occupancy Jackson was constantly called upon to provide overnight lodgings. His was the only stopping place between Cowlitz Landing and Puget Sound. He built several additions to the home and in September, 1862 applied for a hotel license.

At first there were only horse and foot travelers, who brought their own blankets. Mrs. Jackson cooked the meals and the guests spent their evenings in front of the fire in the main room, which also was headquarters for the clerk of the county court and recorder, namely Jackson.

The size of his farm and the scope of his business kept Jackson well occupied until his death in 1873. His widow lived at the house until she passed away in 1900 at the age of 90. After her death the many additions to the main cottage fell in ruins.

Captain Thomas Coupe, whose house follows, was born on the Isle of Man in 1818 and married Maria White, of Bath, Me. in 1840. How he brought his wife to Puget Sound has become almost a legend on Whidbey Island.

The captain sailed to the Pacific in the schooner *Rochester* during the California gold rush in '49 and later bought an interest in the bark *Success*, in which he carried piling from Puget Sound to San Francisco for construction of wharves.

While at Penn's Cove for the purpose of loading timber he took a 320-acre donation land claim in November, 1852 and sent at once for his wife and four children. They arrived on the coast six months later by way of Cape Horn. Captain Coupe picked them up at San Francisco in the *Success* and brought them north. He cast anchor early one morning in Penn's Cove and called, "Mother, come up and see your new home."

The bark was moored almost directly in front of the present site of the house, which is at the east end of Coupeville's waterfront. Indians camped on the beach, there was no dwelling, only a few cleared acres and tall fir trees.

"Is this the place you have brought me to for a

home?" Mrs. Coupe exclaimed in dismay.

"Why, Mother, this is the Garden of Eden," her spouse insisted.

Tradition has it that he then and there promised to leave the sea if she would live on the island.

When the captain went ashore that day he had an unpleasant surprise. A man named Ives had jumped his claim and erected a cabin. Coupe paid him $700 to vacate the property.

For the first year the family lived in the log cabin, then in 1854 the house was ready. Redwood boards, windows, doors, frames, and wainscoting and furnishings were brought in the captain's ship from California. The dwelling formerly stood closer to the water, but crumbling of the bank made it necessary to move it back. Two fireplaces were damaged as a result and had to be walled up.

The two black walnut trees on the property were planted by Captain Coupe.

Another echo of sailing ship days in Coupeville is the Race house on the waterfront adjacent to the city park. It originally stood at Coveland, where it was erected in 1851-2 by Jacob Smith. A few years later Captain James Henry Swift, of New Bedford, commander and part owner of the bark *Anadyr*, called at Camano Island to carry a cargo of spars to Brest for the French navy. The island country appealed to him and in 1857 he purchased the Smith land claim and log house and settled there with his young wife, Emily, six years later.

He said he liked Coupeville because it reminded him of New Bedford. In his day 20 former sea captains were settled around Penn's Cove.

Emily Swift was accustomed to comfortable living and her husband, who made seven voyages around the world, was the man to provide it. The children remembered that their mother wore silks and satins when other mothers in the neighborhood dressed in calicoes.

The family lived in the house a number of years and then moved away. The daughter, Harriet, married Captain F. Puget Race and, when her home on the waterfront site at Coupeville burned, her brother, Dr. George W. Swift, suggested that she buy the old house and move it. Dr. Swift supervised the numbering of the logs and in 1928 the dwelling

was reassembled as it had been. Mrs. Race lived there to the end of her life and upon her death it became the property of Mrs. Swift.

All of the improvements made by Mrs. Race were in complete harmony with the exterior. The old cabin became an ideal setting for her heirloom furniture, dishes and glassware, much of which came around Cape Horn when ships called at Puget Sound for piles and lumber. Other pieces had been brought from the Orient when Captain Swift was on a China run with the *Anadyr*.

The hinges on the front door of the restored cabin are relics of the old Forestry Building at the 1909 Alaska Yukon Pacific Exposition at Seattle.

With the outbreak of the Indian War in 1855 block-houses sprang up all over Western Washington wherever there were small settlements. Most of those surviving today are centered on Whidbey Island, where four may be seen.

The Davis blockhouse, restored in 1931, was built on the donation claim of John Davis, adjoining that of Jacob Ebey, father of Col. Isaac Ebey, who was murdered by raiding Alaskan Indians in 1854. The tragedy occurred on the southwest side of the island, not far away, and spread terror among the settlers' womenfolk.

An interesting feature of the Davis blockhouse is its fireplace with clay and stick chimney. Steps can be seen inside the structure, leading to a ledge where sentinels were posted at port holes.

The entire blockhouse survived well the assaults of time and weather. It required only replacement of some rotted timbers and a new shake roof. The primitive fort stands in Sunnyside Cemetery, where many Whidbey Island pioneers are buried. The descendant of one of them related how her grandmother as a little girl walked through fields of wild flowers to reach the blockhouse and spent happy days there playing with her dolls.

No battles ever were fought around any of these pioneer strongholds, but frightened families took shelter in them at night in times of stress, usually going home in daylight hours to care for their farms.

The Alexander blockhouse in the center of Coupeville once stood in a three-sided stockade on the John Alexander land claim.

This structure has been cared for faithfully by Mrs. Ida Alexander Sill, granddaughter of the widow of Capt. Robert Fay, Whidbey Island's first Indian agent and pioneer fish packer (he had a salmon saltery). After his death Mrs. Fay married John Alexander.

In a case protected by glass to the right of the blockhouse door can be seen a wooden cross erected on the island on May 30, 1840, when the Rev. Father Francis N. Blanchet held the first Catholic services for the Indians roundabout. The cross was carved as a symbol of faith by the tribesmen who prior to Father Blanchet's visit had accepted the white man's religion. The missionary priest baptized 218 persons before leaving the island.

A famous name is associated with Bellingham's oldest structure, the home of Captain (later General) George E. Pickett, celebrated for leading a Confederate charge in the Civil War.

When the house at 910 Bancroft Street was erected in 1858 it did not have the closed porch nor the shingles, added by a later occupant. There were neither time nor materials for making the board-and-batten cottage a stylish home. A ladder at first provided access to the two second-story rooms. A stick-and-mud fireplace furnished heat.

Pickett, a Virginian and a West Pointer, served in the Mexican War and was on duty in Florida when he was sent to the Pacific Coast with troops to protect settlers from Indian depredations. He was nearly seven months at Fort Steilacoom before his assignment to Fort Bellingham. He arrived there in August, 1856 with 68 men of Company D, Ninth Infantry and at once erected a fort three miles northwest of the mouth of Whatcom Creek. Whatcom,

the first community on the bay, was combined with Bellingham in 1903. The dwelling stands in this older section, about 300 feet from the site of a blockhouse in which citizens sought refuge during the Indian scares.

The front room of the house was a center for conducting much official business. Pickett, a widower, had taken as his second wife the daughter of a British Columbia chief. She died shortly after the birth of their son in 1857 and the tiny baby was sent to live with friends in Mason County.

Pickett occupied his residence intermittently, as he was transferred to San Juan Island, then returned to Bellingham and was sent a second time to the island. In June, 1861 he left the Sound to join the Confederate forces.

After his departure the house was occupied for more than half a century by Miss Hattie Strother. Since then it has been the property of the Washington State Historical Society.

In a recently created park near the northwestern tip of San Juan Island, facing Garrison Bay, are two relics of the Pig War, a bloodless conflict between Great Britain and the United States, in which only a porker lost its life.

When tension over ownership of the San Juan Archipelago was at its peak in 1859 the American troops erected a fortification on the south end of the island. British authorities maintained that, with the island in dispute, a similar occupation by English forces was necessary. On March 21, 1860 a company of Royal Marines was landed under command of Captain George Bazalgette. The soldiers set up camp at a previously selected site 11 miles by trail from American headquarters. The captain expected his occupation to be brief, so erected extremely rough cabins.

To give the establishment a military aspect a blockhouse was built. The exact date it was erected is unknown, but it appears in the oldest sketches of the post, with a long wharf and flagpole beside it. The main purpose was to impress raiding Northern Indians, not to defend the British against American attack. The two military units were extremely congenial and their contacts were mainly social.

Several long buildings were on the level ground behind the blockhouse, among them a barrack, still preserved.

Bazalgette waited seven long years in his makeshift camp and still the joint occupation of the island continued. The captain was due for transfer and when it came time for him to leave he recommended that new officers' quarters be erected and the barracks and other buildings repaired. Houses for the captain and doctor went up on the hill and social life took on a gayer aspect. There were theatricals, concerts and balls. One affair on New Year's, 1871 was a supper and dance in the barracks, which were decorated for the occasion with evergreens, holly and flags. Breakfast was served before the guests departed at 7 A.M., escorted part way on the road by the soldiers and their band.

Troops of both nations remained on San Juan until November, 1872. The barracks and commandant's residence (which later burned) were handed over to a representative of the United States Army

and the flagstaff was cut down. The physician's home and one of the barracks burned 15 years later. Gradually the rest fell in ruins, but the blockhouse miraculously survived throughout the years.

A writer in the 1890's told of seeing two barracks standing at right angles at one end of the grassy meadow that had been the parade ground. He said of the place, "When occupied this post must have been one of the most beautiful of all English military stations in the world."

The O. B. McFadden house at 1630 Chehalis Avenue is the oldest building in Chehalis. Two stories high, with eight rooms, it was built for the large family of a leading citizen of Washington Territory. Undoubtedly it has undergone considerable modernization. (See picture on page 27)

Judge Obadiah McFadden was born in Pennsylvania and married there. In 1853 he was appointed circuit judge for Oregon Territory. He covered the western valleys between Vancouver and the Rogue River, riding horseback to court sessions and carrying his documents and law books in saddlebags.

When Washington Territory was formed half a year later he requested to be transferred north of the Columbia, as he was not contented with his role in Oregon, due to having replaced an extremely popular judge. He was given the first district, consisting of Walla Walla, Skamania, Clark, Cowlitz, Wahkiakum and Pacific Counties. This again meant much traveling for him.

Before taking the appointment he went home to see his family. Mrs. McFadden no longer could endure the separation, so he brought her and their seven children to Fort Vancouver. He purchased the south half of the Schuyler S. Saunders donation claim at Saundersville (Chehalis) and had Saunders build the large log house for him. The place was reached only by trails and Mrs. McFadden had to accustom herself to living in the wilderness. Friends back East had frightened her with stories of Indian attacks.

When the end of McFadden's term drew near he was the only judge reappointed. He became the territory's second chief justice and held office until March, 1861 when President Lincoln displaced all of the judges. McFadden by then had been seven

years on Washington Territory's bench. He next became interested in territorial legislation, was a senator in 1862 and on July 4 of that year presided at a mass meeting at Claquato so persuasively that it influenced Washington's determination to remain in the union. The judge was reelected to the territorial legislature in 1863 and 1864 and presided over a session. He had gone back to the practice of law and opened an office in Olympia. In 1873 he was elected Delegate to Congress and died two years later in Olympia, shortly after his term expired. He was 61.

He had 10 children. Mrs. McFadden died in 1903 in the home the family had moved into in Olympia.

Judge McFadden was popular, a firm yet gentle man, never unkind or abrupt, genial, companionable and with a keen sense of humor. Chehalis named a park for him.

The house there has been occupied almost continuously since it was built. Upon the death of Saunders, who had been postmaster, the post office was transferred to this dwelling and about that time the name of the settlement was changed to Chehalis. This must have been about when the McFaddens moved to Olympia.

As a town Claquato was older than its larger neighbor, Chehalis, a few miles to the east. It was founded in 1853 by Lewis H. Davis and became a way station on the early Military Road. For a time it was the largest community between Olympia and the Columbia River, having a sawmill and grist mill, general store, small hotel, stables, blacksmith, carpenter shop and post office.

Davis owned the mill and donated the first lumber it produced for construction in 1858 of a church that is standing there yet, the second oldest Protestant church in Washington. Other residents of the village gave labor or supplies. Nails were forged by the local blacksmith. Mrs. Davis' brother, John Duff Clinger, supervised construction and fashioned the doors and window casings.

The design was copied from the First Methodist Church of Portland, though on a smaller scale. The sanctuary is 20 by 23 feet, with a small room at the rear. Most striking feature is the crown of thorns surmounting the louvered belfry.

Pews, pulpit and pastor's chair were the work of the Boisfort community a few miles away and were a gift. The old bell, cast by Henry A. Hooper & Co. of Boston in 1857, hangs in the tower.

The Rev. John F. Devore, a Methodist circuit rider, conducted the initial services and John Harwood became the first resident minister. The latter was Claquato's first schoolteacher. He held classes in a log cabin, after which he moved the pupils into the new building and made it serve a double purpose. With arrival of the railroad in the '70's the population shifted to Chehalis and a new school on Newaukum River superseded the "academy."

The first bride who lived in the commandant's house at Fort Simcoe State Park in Yakima County was Marianna Nelson Garnett, wife of Maj. Robert Selden Garnett. He had established the military post in August, 1856 during the Indian War. The first quarters were of pine logs, but, with a permanent installation planned, the Army freighted in doors, sashes, mantels, book cases and equipment for building comfortable officers' quarters. Bricks were made on the spot and were employed liberally between the studding for insulation.

Garnett, a Virginian and a West Pointer, had been aide de camp to Gen. Zachary Taylor and accompanied him to Washington, D.C. for the latter's inauguration as President. The major returned to the East during his first winter at the fort and married Marianna in New York. He brought her back with him in May, 1857 and in less than a year she gave birth to an infant son. In writing to friends about the baby she spoke of her place of residence as "a very pretty and conveniently arranged house."

While the major was absent from home with his troops on a 31-day march Mrs. Garnett and the baby died of a fever. The child was seven months and five days old. It was a sad return for the commanding officer. He accompanied the bodies to

New York, but came back again and remained at the fort until it was transferred to the Indian Department May 22, 1859. After that the house was occupied by a succession of Indian agents.

Garnett resigned from the United States Army in April, 1861 to become an officer in the Confederacy. He was killed in action.

His home today is a museum, furnished with relics of the Indian War period. Its exterior style was the then-new American Gothic.

LOG CABINS

As soon as a pioneer arrived and selected the land where he was to live he began felling trees, clearing brush and leveling the spot where his house was to stand. Logs were cut the correct length for walls and notched at the corners. A fireplace and chimney were built with the easiest materials at hand, most often clay and sticks.

If the family owned a crane it was installed, so that kettles might be hung over the fire, which served for heating and cooking and to a certain extent for light.

Windows might be mere openings in the logs covered with a thinly scraped deerhide or oiled paper or a wooden shutter until glass could be obtained.

An example of the interior of such early homes is in the Cowlitz County Museum at Kelso, where a cabin of the type current in 1853 was reassembled after being moved from its site on the Toutle River. Members of the county historical society searched for suitable furnishings. Here one can see a towel, hand woven of home-grown flax, a bootjack, black iron griddle, iron kettle, earthenware jars for food storage, candle snuffer, cradle, candle mold, coffee mill and many other utilitarian articles. Every piece has a history and many date back to the wagon-train period.

The settler who lived in a cabin as complete as this enjoyed more than ordinary comfort. The striped rag rug on the puncheon floor was indeed a refinement. Pioneers often had to make do with Indian mats woven from reeds.

Members of the society wore old costumes when posing for this picture.

Not all log cabins were constructed by experts, nor were the tools equal to those of a modern cabin-builder's kit. An ax often constituted a man's entire equipment and his principal aim was to provide himself with shelter under primitive conditions. He usually thought of the cabin as a temporary expedient.

Such construction is an old folk art of timbered countries. Swedes introduced it into Delaware in colonial times and the method quickly spread westward across the mountains.

Log cabins actually belong to no single period of Washington's history. They were the first shelters and they are still being built today as vacation homes, hunting and woodsmen's shacks.

A description survived of Americans building some of their initial housing in the Pacific Northwest in this account of a missionary in 1834:

"The rainy season was fast approaching and a house was wanted to shelter us . . . . But first we had to prepare our tools . . . We handled axes and augurs, hung a grindstone. . . . Our house advanced but slowly and we were caught in one violent storm of wind and rain, which was near drenching all we had, the tent which we occupied being but a poor protection. . . . Before the next storm came on we had a roof on a part of our house and a piece of floor laid, on which we could lie thankfully secure from the pelting storm without. A few weeks, all the time hard at it, and the roof was completed; a good chimney made of sticks and clay, and a fireplace in one end; floors laid of plank split from fir and hewn on the upper side; doors procured in the same way and hung on wooden hinges. Then a table, then stools and finally the luxury of chairs added to our self-made comforts. Our good mansion, 20 by 30 feet, divided into two apartments by a partition across the window, and lighted by four small windows, the sashes partly made . . . with a jackknife."

So much for the way the missionaries did it; we have an idea that the Barker cabin, now at Federal Way shopping center, south of Seattle, was much less of an ordeal to erect.

Whatever its true background, the cabin below, moved from the White River Valley and re-erected at Federal Way shopping center on Highway 99 south of Seattle, is an authentic specimen of a very old type. Its owners believe it was one of a string of cabins built by the Hudson's Bay Co. to strengthen its claims to land in the 1850's. An old resident, however, declared it was the hop house of Jeremiah Stilley, who settled in the vicinity of Buckley in 1870. A newspaper, dated 1862 and found pasted on the cabin wall, further complicated guesswork about the building's identity.

Though the cabin's beginning is obscure, it is conceded by experts that the ax work on the mortised corners is more in the style of Hudson's Bay Co. construction than the average American pioneer's workmanship. Stilley, a native of Ohio, was attracted to British Columbia by the Fraser River gold rush and on his return was employed four years as a carpenter by the Puget Sound Agricultural Co., which had headquarters at Fort Nisqually. When he gravitated to the Auburn and Puyallup area a few years later he may have been influenced by his former employers' mode of building.

Several cabins of this type stood near the White River in early days and were so old that no one was certain of their history. They may have been erected for the purpose of holding claims. Some are known to have been put up for the company between the Nisqually and Puyallup Rivers, but it is

doubtful if the British had any intention of claiming land beyond these boundary streams. Many land-seekers roved through the country in quest of donation claims, but turned faint-hearted and departed before they proved up on their forested areas.

Almost unchanged since it was built in 1859, the Ransom Clark log cabin, on the H. A. Reynolds farm south of Walla Walla, is an excellent example of a pioneer's home. Only the fireplace and chimney are missing from it. The structure has been used for storage of tools and produce and no attempt has been made to alter it. The two rooms inside are separated by a dog-trot or breezeway, which later was closed with a wall or door.

This arrangement was favored by settlers from some parts of the Midwest and was achieved by building two cabins under a common roof extending over the space between them. One cabin would be used for sleeping, the other for kitchen, dining and general living.

Ransom Clark filed on a 640-acre donation claim in 1855 and was in the Blue Mountains cutting logs for his house when the order went out that because of Indian troubles all settlers were to leave the Walla Walla Valley. Three years passed before he was permitted to return. On starting back to his land Clark secured eight boxes of fruit-tree grafts and he and his 13-year-old son drove them in a wagon from The Dalles. The pair lived in a tent until their home was built with logs. Clark paid for the timbers with young trees from his nursery or with his services as plowman.

Leaving the boy and a friend to care for the place, Clark returned to Portland to fetch his wife and younger son. Before he could return the homesteader fell sick with fever and died suddenly.

Mrs. Clark, who was expecting another child, courageously decided to take a look at the farm. She was satisfied with what she saw and concluded to stay. But first she returned to Portland for the birth of her daughter. She brought her two small children to Walla Walla by stagecoach and set about proving up on the claim. To earn a living she milked, made butter, gardened and sewed flour sacks for the Simms-Dent flour mill.

During this period she became acquainted with Almos Reynolds, a millwright, and the couple were married at the cabin on May 23, 1861. The farm remained continuously in the family ever since, though a modern residence took the place of the cabin, a treasured souvenir of other days. Soon, however, it is to be moved to the Fort Walla Walla Park museum complex for its pioneer village, having been given for that purpose.

The Paul Kintschi home near Edwall is a remodelled stage station on the old Colville military road from Walla Walla. This pioneer highway ran from Wallula on the Columbia River to Walla Walla, thence across the Snake at Lyons Ferry and on north to the Colville Valley, where Major Pinckney Lugenbeel in 1859 erected an Army post. When gold was discovered in the Canadian Kootenays the route was heavily travelled and much freighting was done.

The two-story roadhouse was erected in 1868 by a man named Wood. Hand-hewed pine logs, 11 inches square, were used for the outside walls. For heating there was a fireplace and chimney of large rocks. Formerly the downstairs was one large room and only the sleeping quarters on the upper floor had partitions.

The grandfather of the present owner homesteaded about four miles away and, when Mrs. Wood lost the house to a mortgage company, Mrs. Kintschi's uncle, John Vogel, bought it in 1906. It has belonged to some member of the same family ever since, the last previous owner being Mrs. Kintschi's mother, Mrs. Adelhied McRae.

Except for an enlarged window in the living room and evidence of such electrical equipment as a TV mast, the exterior is not greatly changed since horse-drawn stages galloped up to the door.

An important new acquisition of the Washington Parks and Recreation Commission is the 217-acre Olmstead homestead on Squaw Creek Trail Road, a few miles out of Ellensburg. It includes a cabin erected in 1875 and a later home dating from 1907.

The cabin, carefully sheltered under a shed roof, is furnished with rag rugs, chairs, dishes and articles belonging to the period when Samuel Bedient Olmstead, a Civil War veteran, went to the Kittitas Valley with his wife and three children, riding horseback over the Snoqualmie trail from Seattle.

He built his cabin of cottonwood trees cut in Yakima Canyon and hauled in a lynchpin wagon to the site. He squared the logs with a broad ax and dovetailed them at the corners. Wooden pegs and square iron nails, hand-made in the local blacksmith shop, held the house together. The roof was of shakes, the doors fastened by iron staples and a wooden bar. The living room fireplace was put together of sticks and mud. The window glass was brought from The Dalles.

The cabin is 24 feet square and has three rooms, with a shed on the south side used for a summer kitchen and in winter as a store room. A port hole in the north wall is a reminder of the Indian troubles of 1877 and 1878, when neighbors gathered at the cabin at night for mutual protection.

Olmstead family history goes back to the Puritans and to a Revolutionary War general. Clareta Olmstead Smith and Leta May Smith, granddaughters of Samuel and Sarah Olmstead, have been officers of the D.A.R. and active in patriotic organizations and historical societies, so all the years they have lived on the farm they have been desirous of preserving their heritage. In September, 1968 they deeded both houses and all of the articles in them to the state for an historical park and recreational center.

The second oldest building in Kittitas County is the cabin built by "Cayuse" Mes Jenson, Harry Masterson, Howard Masterson and Chris Anderson in the fall of 1882 or the spring of 1883 at Roslyn.

Jenson homesteaded 160 acres where the town lies and the first winter he was on the property John Stone, a trapper, lived with him. Stone was the first man to find coal in the area, discovering an outcrop near the Jenson ranch. Jenson hauled this coal to Ellensburg with his team and wagon and sold the fuel to Jake Becker for his blacksmith shop. Thereafter Jenson made fortnightly trips from the mines to supply Ellensburg blacksmiths.

His log cabin stands at the corner of North Second and Utah Streets.

Inside this ugly shed north of Oroville is the log cabin of Okanogan County's first settler. This is an unconventional way in which to preserve a relic of a venerated citizen, but the log house is there for those who care to inspect it.

Hiram Francis Smith, a native of Maine, worked as a printer on New York newspapers until the California gold rush lured him west in 1849. He followed the gold rush to the Caribou in British Columbia in 1858 and that same year built a cabin near Lake Osoyoos. He opened an outfitting headquarters for miners, took an Indian wife and became a permanent resident.

Smith attained fame when, as a member of the 1865-66 territorial legislature he introduced a bill petitioning Congress to obtain concessions in Russian America which would enable American cod and halibut-fishing vessels to visit ports there to ob-

tain fuel, water and provisions. His was a timely move which may have started the ball rolling toward the purchase of Alaska the following year.

In 1892 Smith served another term in the legislature. He died in 1893.

Largely because of him, when a reservation was designated for Chief Moses' tribe in 1872, President Grant signed a document setting aside a 15-mile strip down the Okanogan River, which was left open to mineral entry. It fixed an inviolate guardianship of Smith's ranch. To this day one of the proudest names in the county is that of "Okanogan" Smith.

Wenatchee has a landmark in the Samuel Miller cabin, which besides providing a home for the owner, was the first trading post and post office in the valley. It was erected in 1872 near the north end of Miller Street and was moved to its present site near the approach to the highway bridge across the Columbia in 1959. It no longer looks like the same cabin in old photographs.

Sam Miller arrived in Wenatchee in 1871 and lived there 35 years. He was born in Ohio in 1828, crossed the plains in 1853 to California and in 1862 went to Walla Walla. There he joined in partnership with Frank and David Freer to establish a freight line from Wallula to the Florence, Idaho mines. The men ran 100 pack mules and prospered until freight wagons and roads put them out of business. They turned their attention toward the north and decided to establish a trading business with the Indians in the Columbia Valley. Very con-

veniently they were able to buy out one at Wenatchee started by two men who were threatened with arrest for selling liquor to Indians.

After the Freer brothers died, Miller managed their estates and took care of their families. He survived until 1906.

It was a great event in the valley when Miller became postmaster; the settlers said it gave them a metropolitan feeling; they could now receive mail without a long journey to pick it up.

Some log houses were constructed more carefully than others, with squared logs and mortised joints. They were tight enough so that they could be papered or plastered inside.

Here is such a neatly made house, constructed entirely without the use of nails. It was built at Chewelah in 1868 for an Indian agency and was purchased from the government in 1902 by Dr. S. P. McPherson, who also bought a granary at the same time from the federal authorities and combined the two for his family's living quarters.

The house fell into disuse for a number of years, but Mrs. Alice Salisbury, the physician's daughter, felt that so old a building should be saved, so she rehabilitated it and lives there. She removed the granary portion, which was in bad condition, and the building is now like its former state. It is one story, divided into three rooms where formerly there was but a single large chamber.

Years ago the family found in the attic papers of the Indian agency, which were given to Washington State University.

On state highway property south of the entrance to Soap Lake are the remains of the Jack Splawn cabin, moved from the Priest Rapids Dam area, where it was erected in 1873. The dwelling, one of the first in present Grant County, is proof that the log cabin is among the simplest forms of housing. The logs in it must have been brought or drifted some distance down river before Splawn pulled them in to the bank and converted them into his home on the Figure Two ranch.

Splawn ran vast herds of cattle, said to have reached as high as 125,000 head. He conducted drives to the Fraser River mines, taking fresh meat on the hoof to the argonauts.

The cabin was in use until the dam was constructed and the reservoir filled in 1957. Splawn lived there only until about 1900. It was used later by an irrigation development company. Descendants of Splawn gave the building and $350 toward its restoration to the Grant County Historical Society. A plan is under consideration to develop it as a tourist attraction.

Sunnyside's city park has for an attraction the first white man's cabin built in the Yakima Valley. As it was moved in 1953 from its former site seven miles south of town and preserved under a shed, Ben Snipes, the pioneer of 1859, might have difficulty recognizing it, were his ghostly embodiment able to roam again the cattle trails of Central Washington.

Snipes was considered the greatest of Northwest cattle men in the open-range period. He drove a herd from The Dalles to the Fraser River miners of British Columbia on his initial trek through the valley. He returned five years later and established a camp six miles from present Toppenish and another near Granger. His brother-in-law, H. H. Allen, joined him and they ran thousands of head of cattle over a vast territory. Snipes' herd, like that of Splawn, once numbered 125,000.

As Ben prospered he opened banks at Ellensburg and Roslyn. They were closed in the panic of 1893, which marked collapse of the Snipes empire.

BEN SNIPE'S CABIN
THE FIRST WHITEMANS
CABIN IN THE YAKIMA
VALLEY - BUILT IN

The Longmire cabin is the only remaining structure reminiscent of the first settlement in present Mount Rainier National Park.

James Longmire led a wagon train in 1853 over the Oregon Trail, the first to cross the Columbia River near Walla Walla and to penetrate the Cascade Mountains by way of the Yakima and Wenas Valleys. Crossing to the south side of the Nisqually River, the party arrived at Yelm Prairie, where the family settled.

Not long afterward Longmire went looking for a better passage through the range than Naches Pass and about 1859 or a little later he hacked out a trail from Yelm to Bear Prairie. In 1870 he was employed by P. B. Van Trump and Hazard Stevens to lead the first conquerors of the mountain to its base. Later that year he guided the S. F. Emmons—A. D. Wilson party. In 1883 Longmire made the climb to the top himself, accompanying Van Trump, and at that time Longmire mineral springs were discovered. This gave James the idea of establishing a mineral claim and building a hotel. He filed on a homestead of 640 acres and in 1884 began improvements. By the following year tourists were being accommodated at the log inn.

Longmire must have discovered he could not receive title to so much land and in 1887 he located a mineral claim on slightly less than 20 acres, based on mineral paint and auriferous gravel.

The family aided the endeavor and James' eldest son, Elcaine, constructed the small log cabin near the Iron Mike spring in 1888. A two-story hotel was constructed in 1890.

At first it was intended to use the cabin as a meat house, then Elcaine's boys lived in it summers. Most of the family occupied tents until the hotel was built. The cabin furnishings were simple, consisting of a stove and a bunk, stool and table made of tree limbs.

The cabin was only a small part of the Longmires' medical spa, but it is all that remains of it. There were more springs in that day, but road improvements have destroyed some.

Most of the place names around the park originated with the Longmires and many of the trails were blazed by them. After James died in 1897 management fell to Elcaine and his children. The park was created at the turn of the century, when the Longmire operation was at its height. Elcaine died in 1915 and this ended the family's association with the park.

The cabin does not look exactly as in early photographs because of minor repairs and general maintenance. This accounts, too, for wire nails hammered into the building to hold bark or siding to the log walls and the presence of a new door.

As a homestead cabin the structure merely served for proving up on the mineral placer claim.

In Pioneer Park at Ferndale are two old cabins, the first of which was moved to town more than 20 years ago. It was erected in 1895 near Lake Whatcom and had long been deserted. It was donated as a pioneer memorial and became the nucleus of the village which the Pioneer Society expects to assemble in the park.

The society now has a church dating from 1875 and will equip a store. The cabins are furnished with period pieces, but not with articles of the former owners.

The second cabin acquired was the Conrad Shields house, built early in the 1880's on the Guide Road near Wiser Lake. Shields, born in Hesse, Germany in 1832, was a carpenter, as were some of his sons. Evidence of his skill is to be seen in the dovetailing of the corner joints of the squared logs throughout the house.

At the north entrance to Pioneer Park, LaConner is a cabin which Magnus Anderson erected in 1869 near the north fork of the Skagit River. It was given by S. B. Miller to the Daughters of the Pioneers of Washington and moved and restored by that organization.

Anderson was the first Scandinavian to settle in Skagit County, homesteading 160 acres. He was born in Sweden and made several trips around Cape Horn as a ship's carpenter before taking up land in 1869.

His initial farming was done by hand, later with oxen. He had the first horses in the area and made history when he drove the team and wagon to Mount Vernon. It was necessary to carry his ax, saw, peavey and shovel in order to clear the route of brush and logs.

Anderson brought his bride by rowboat from LaConner to his 12-by-20-foot log house in 1873.

Tacoma's first house was a log cabin standing today in Point Defiance Park, where it was moved from the foot of McCarver Street. For many years this was the home of Job Carr, who arrived on the south side of Tacoma Bay by canoe in Christmas week, 1864, when no white men as yet lived there. Upon finding an area where there were no high banks fronting on the water he took a claim and speedily built a cabin. His two sons staked other claims nearby.

The Carrs made no effort to plat a town, but they were not long undisturbed. A railroad boom was in the making and General Morton Mathew McCarver in 1868 came overland from Portland on horseback, looking for a townsite that might appeal to the Northern Pacific for a terminus. He persuaded Carr to sell the land at $10 per acre, all but five acres where his house and garden were. McCarver homesteaded another claim and located one for a brother of his partner in the venture.

It is interesting that Job Carr at the age of 70 prospected for a bride through a correspondence bureau. Miss Addie Emery arrived from New York in response to his proposal and they were married

in Olympia in 1884. He lived only three years longer.

To the day of his death Carr and many others believed there was a gold deposit on Mount Rainier known to an Indian who brought a pouch of nuggets to town from time to time and exchanged them for liquor. Carr went searching for the source and, when met on the north side of the mountain, was most secretive. It is believed, however, that he never found the golden treasure.

When in 1956 the Orcas Island Historical Society was seeking a place in which to house its accumulation of relics and papers which were being stored in a private home, a pioneer cabin was offered to the group. The abandoned house was then 71 years old and had been the home of John Boede and his family. The stipulation was that it would have to be dismantled and moved to property the society owned.

Members conceived the idea of using the cabin as a nucleus for a group of similar structures. Soon three more were acquired and the work of moving and restoring them was placed in charge of Walter Hall, president of the organization and a former engineering instructor. All the cabins needed new roofs and Hall had them made of hand-cut shakes. Logs needing to be replaced were hand-sawed like the originals.

The fireplace in the Boede cabin was an addition, built by Hall with brick salvaged from the early-day Kimple brickyard at West Beach.

The museum exhibits reflect what life was like in the San Juans half a century or more ago.

Under the auspices of the Clallam County Historical Society, the L. L. Beaumont cabin on South Mount Angeles Road was moved to the grounds of the Olympic Park Pioneer Memorial Museum in Port Angeles and was restored with contributions of labor and period furnishings. It is open to visitors during museum hours.

The cabin was built in 1887 when only a trail existed where the road now passes. The same family occupied it almost 40 years, staying on after proving up on a 160-acre homestead.

In 1967 the George Thomas Richardson cabin was brought from Monitor to the Old Mission Village at Cashmere, the second time the house was moved since its erection in 1886. Seven sons of the family were born in it before the dwelling was transferred from a bench south of Monitor to another part of the Richardson orchard to make room for a large frame home built in 1900.

The cabin dates from before creation of Chelan County. The Richardsons spent four days traveling to Monitor from Ellensburg, trailing their cow and calf. They followed an old Indian route. When they reached the Wenatchee River it was so high they left the wagon four miles away and walked in. Next day they borrowed an additional team and went for the wagon.

That first summer the family lived in a tent. The father went freighting to earn the wherewithal for starting his home. He built the house on a rock foundation. The logs were cut with a broad ax, the corners mortised and a wooden peg inserted. The

only nails were square-headed ones in the roof. A crude stairway led to the one-room loft.

Richardson did dry farming on his 160 acres. He planted fruit trees in 1889, carrying water to them from the river. Two years later he constructed a water wheel to help with irrigation. Before his orchard came into bearing he raised sorghum and traded syrup for necessities.

Monitor was called Brown's Flat until Richardson, with patriotic thoughts about the Monitor and the Merrimac, suggested the present name at a community meeting.

Displayed in the house at present are several original furnishings of the Richardsons, among them a tall screened cupboard, black pots, a stone jug and flat iron.

Another of the cabins in Cashmere's historic park is that of Michael Horan, who lived in the house from 1896 to 1900 when it stood at the confluence of the Columbia and Wenatchee Rivers.

Horan, born in Stockbridge, Mass. in 1854, received a good education before he left home for California in 1876. Eight years later he went to Tacoma and operated a stone quarry. His next move was to Wenatchee in the spring of 1889, a few months after his marriage. He started a meat business, weathering an extremely hard winter when hay was so scarce in the valley it brought $50 a ton when any was available. Snow was up to the second strand of barbed wire fences and the Wenatchee River was frozen its entire length. Even the Columbia was frozen in places.

That spring it was common to see settlers bringing in a few forksful of grass gathered from the southern exposure of some cliff—anything to keep the cattle alive. Flour was short and bacon rinds were cherished food. The situation was saved when a load of supplies was freighted over the mountains from Ellensburg.

Men had to go away from the valley in those days to work for a grubstake, Horan harvesting

wheat south of Walla Walla in order to have funds to carry him through.

Horan told of the problems of getting water on the land so that crops could be grown. "If we put our water wheels too near the bank the summer drought would leave them dry," he recalled. "If we put them too far in the channel, the spring flood would wash them away."

His second winter in the valley the weather was more open, the bunch grass was within easy reach and the mountains were not so difficult to cross. Wenatchee commenced to thrive in the spring of 1892 when the coming of the Great Northern Railroad was imminent.

Horan very soon prospered by contracting for large deliveries of meat to construction crews.

Horan was a member of Wenatchee's first city council. When he died in 1919 his widow went on living at the old ranch. The Horans had six children, one of whom, Walter, was elected to Congress.

Not plush residences but mining community abodes were this log cabin and the back room of an abandoned office building in Chesaw, Okanogan County. Settled by men who rushed in to homestead free land on the opening of the northern half of the Colville Indian Reservation, the town was boomed by discovery of gold in 1896 on streams in the vicinity. A tent city at first, it thrived and log cabins went up. The population reached 500 before the gold deposits were exhausted and Chesaw became a ghost town.

This venerable cabin in the northwestern corner of Ferry County is associated with the name of Ranald McDonald, the first American to visit Japan. He died on August 5, 1894 in the log house at the confluence of Toroda Creek and Kettle River and is buried nearby.

McDonald was the son of Archibald McDonald, a Hudson's Bay Co. trader, and a Chinook Indian princess. Ranald was born in Astoria in 1824 and was educated in Eastern Canada. He went to sea as a young man and in 1848 asked to be set ashore in Japan. He was arrested immediately and kept in prison. While there he taught English to Japanese who later served as court interpreters.

Ranald was rescued, taken to the China coast and later went to Australia, where he mined gold. He returned to the Pacific Northwest, stayed for a while in British Columbia, then homesteaded in Stevens County, Wash. He never married and when he became sick at Kettle Falls his niece, Mrs. Jennie Lynch, brought him to Toroda, where she lived in the squared-log house.

It had been built on land traditionally occupied by her grandmother's people, members of the Okanogan tribe of Indians. Ranald's half brother, Ben McDonald, met Mrs. Lynch's grandmother at Osoyoos Lake, where he was associated with John

Utz, builder of the cabin known as the first American custom house at that point.

When McDonald married the Okanogan girl they all moved to the valley at Kettle River and the men in 1869 erected the two old cabins to be seen there. The McDonalds lived in the two-story one.

The family remained behind after Ben McDonald went off to the Cariboo gold rush and struck it rich. He sent Jennie away to mission school, where she remained 18 years. Meanwhile her mother married again.

Jennie became Mrs. George Nelson. She persuaded her husband to go with her to Kettle River so that she might again live there. They bought rights to the property from an uncle, who had inherited it. Nelson was killed accidentally shortly after that and Jennie met and married Jim Lynch.

When she heard that her father's half brother, Ranald, was sick at the old Hudson's Bay post she brought him to the log house and cared for him to the end.

The two cabins and the house, which Jim Lynch built before 1900 on the property, are still in the family, owned by Jennie's grandson, Lewis Stanton. Ownership of the ranch actually has belonged to his people since the Okanogans first came to the valley, long before arrival of the white fur traders.

This house, erected in the spring of 1896, is believed the first built in the Eureka gold mining camp, present Republic. When the north half of the Colville Indian Reservation was opened for prospecting and mineral entry in February, 1896 Harry Kaufman, an Easterner who had been at the older Conconully camp, went to the new location and built himself neat quarters.

With the platting of the town of Republic the thoroughfare in front of his cabin became Kaufman Street. Later Harry and Nellie Miller for many years occupied the home. Their heirs gave it to the Ferry County Historical Society, with $100 toward the cost of moving the cabin to a site behind the Ferry County Courthouse, where it now stands. Displays related to early mining, logging and homesteading will be placed there.

The cabin is slightly different from the usual run. Its squared timbers are finished with uprights at the corners and the gable ends of the house are shingled.

Oroville's log custom house, built about 1890 and still in fair condition, is rented as a residence. It was constructed to provide living quarters for the inspector at this lonely frontier.

The first customs house at this point, built two miles up the east side of Osoyoos Lake, north of Oroville, in the 1870's was also a log cabin. It stood very close to the ranch of famous "Okanogan" Smith. The building was torn down about 1938 and the timbers were used to crib a cellar.

British Columbia also had a log house for its customs inspectors, stationed at Osoyoos, six miles from Oroville. One of the old Canadian cabins has been made into a local historical museum.

Some cabins in Okanogan County are abandoned, such as the one shown on page 2 at the old mining camp of Gilbert.

Here and there a cabin still is lived in, such as this pensioner's home overlooking the river valley at Methow. The structure originally stood at Squaw Creek, but was moved in recent years. The squared logs perhaps were more neatly mortised at the corners before the radical change of location was made.

The Fontaine cabin at Molson was built in 1898 by a bachelor prospector and blacksmith who came from Camp McKinney, B.C., a few miles north of there.

Frank Fontaine staked mining claims on the American side of the border about a mile and a half north of what was to become Molson. In 1900, when the north half of the Colville Reservation opened, he filed a homestead or squatter's right on his mining claims.

In December, 1902 John and Amanda Sherling

and their sons, Ernest and Harry, moved into the cabin. Sherling had bought Fontaine's right to the property.

The cabin was 12 by 16 feet in size, with a dirt floor and earth roof, later replaced with a board floor and shingles.

lived for three years while her husband worked in

In this tiny house Mrs. Sherling and her boys Canadian mines to make their living.

The cabin was in continual use until 1920, though it was enlarged with a frame addition. After the property was sold the old house was abandoned. Harry Sherling bought it in 1962 and next year moved it to the site of Old Molson, which has been developed into a pioneer museum.

Though the Fontaine house was not the first cabin in the area, Sherling says it is the oldest one left.

Guy Waring arrived in the Upper Methow Valley in 1891 and set up a store, organizing the Methow Trading Co. A peeled-log house on Castle Avenue in Winthrop, now the S. W. Shafer Museum, is generally credited with having been Waring's, although he had an earlier house which burned down.

Any building associated with Waring has an aura of romance. He was a member of the Harvard University class of 1882 and when he first moved west in 1884 he bought a squatter's right 12 miles south of the border. This location proved too lonely for his family, so they went East again. Waring returned in 1891 and this time chose Winthrop for his home because of the prospectors who were thronging to both branches of the Methow River. He named the town after Governor Winthrop of Massachusetts. At first Waring's was the only store on the Methow. His company established a chain of branches, with prospectors, miners and trappers as patrons.

Waring was a friend of Owen Wister, who visited him and completed his book, "The Virginian," while there. Wister wrote another story, "Where It Was," appearing in the Saturday Evening Post about 1910, with scenes and characters from Winthrop. In it the storekeeper was the counterpart of Waring.

To all the country roundabout Waring was known as "the man at the forks." The house he built in 1897 on the bluff became in later years an Episcopal church.

When S. W. Shafer, another Winthrop merchant, retired in 1944 and wanted a place to accommodate his collection of pioneer furnishings he purchased the structure and moved in his antique organs, firearms, gold pans, carriage lamps and the like. He continued to make additions to the collection until his death ten years later.

On Puget Sound many of the carpenters were from New England and brought an architectural pattern familiar to them, simple frame houses one or two stories high. You can still see surviving examples attached to the rear of a farmhouse, amid a row of crumbling structures on a down-graded side street or among the blackberry thickets on an abandoned ranch.

It was common to have the back wing the oldest part of a house and the main one added to it. Sometimes a newer porch partially concealed the old wing.

Early carpenters groped their way around. They did not have much information, but were influenced by the classic in developing their own style. They brought molding knives and made the trims themselves. A favorite roof finish was a strong overhanging eave, horizontal at the ends of the gutters—what we have called a returned cornice. This was a modification of the classical cornice.

House builders were conservative and wanted no change from the established patterns of other parts of the country. There was not a graduate architect in the United States until 1873. Those who designed the homes of the Pacific Northwest often were surveyors, railroad builders, cabinet makers, engineers or ship carpenters.

Pattern books filled a real need in that day of no trained designers and no architectural magazines.

After the simple houses of very early years we had those with a front gable and the beginning of gingerbread. The Gothic type began to appear in the 1860's and within another decade there was a tendency to try and make any house look like a mansion, with bay windows, many small porches, deep and heavily bracketed cornices and towers. Next came the French Second Empire style with a mansard roof, which never became very popular here. Nevertheless some outstanding examples survive.

While we never had Gothic stone mansions because of their cost, we had carpenter Gothic, the same style translated into wood, with steep gables, pointed windows and scroll-sawed gingerbread instead of stone tracery.

Then came the English styles—Elizabethan, Jacobean and Queen Anne. About 1890-91 these reached the height of extravagant detail, the flowering of the Victorian age, when curlicues, flourishes and frills were part of every aspect of living. Towers were piled on towers, there were chimneys of all dimensions, scalloped shingles, jigsaw fretwork, dormers and cupalos, small diamond window panes and colored glass. Sometimes they were all mixed together on a single house.

Whidbey Island

A gap was bridged in the 1850's between log houses and those of milled lumber. Such a structure is the Wanamaker or Robertson house, on Coupeville's Front Street, where the squared hand-hewn timbers in the foot-thick walls are concealed under clapboards. The dwelling originally consisted of two front rooms with ceilings 11 feet high. The right-hand room was intended for Captain William Robertson's horse-powered grist mill.

Mrs. J. W. Rosenfield, who owns the place, said that her late husband, a builder, was able to trace the changes in the house. First the room for the mill was completed, then the left-hand front room and the hall. After that the entire back portion, 60 feet wide, was added. In the attic the heavy squared logs of the main house are still visible. The downstairs rooms were finished with tongue-and-groove cedar boards, covered with cheese-cloth and papered. John Rosenfield would have liked to remove this coating and leave the cedar as interior finishing, but he found too many nail holes in it.

The beautiful front door with four panels and sidelights was installed by John Robertson, the mill owner's son, when the structure was converted into a dwelling.

No real history of the house has been traced, but a record of 1864 mentions that the Robertson mill was hired for court purposes from the time the building was completed, with an option to buy. An 1863 description of the town says that between Captain Coupe's house and the village there were only woods and a narrow wagon road. "There were no houses between the two places until you got to John Robertson's general store in a small one-story building in the back part of which was a bar." The

only other buildings in Coupeville at the time were a two-story structure with a hall and Captain Robert Fay's large log house.

Coupeville residents no longer associate the Robertson name with the house. In 1900 it was purchased by a widow, Mrs. Sarah E. Wanamaker, mother of Mrs. Rosenfield. Few changes were made in it except for lowering the ceilings to make heating easier. The original windows with 12 panes remain in most of the house; one can distinguish the bubbles in the old glass.

This view of Coupeville's Front Street is taken from the Rosenfield's porch. The building housing the Jules Cafe was once the Robertson grocery.

With its large areas of plate glass, this does not suggest one of Whidbey Island's oldest residences, yet it is second oldest and, not only that, it served as the island's pioneer court house.

The building stands at San de Fuca at the head of Penn's Cove and faces the main island highway connecting Coupeville and Oak Harbor. Formerly a pair of windows was on either side of the front entrance and none in the end except small panes in the lean-to section. The shutters upstairs are a modern accessory. Formerly there was a chimney at both ends of the roof.

The house dates from 1855, two years after Grennan and Cranney, owners of the Utsalady sawmill, opened a store at the head of the cove in a log cabin. The two-story house replaced the cabin and was of ample size to accommodate both store and living quarters. Here too the district court convened.

In its earliest years the lower floor was of puncheons. Walls and ceilings were covered with cheesecloth, over which were pasted layers of magazines and newspapers. Before the place was modernized one could find pages on the walls dated 1866. The exterior timber walls later were concealed by siding and, more recently, by plastic shingles.

The hand-split shake roof lasted until 1944, when it had to be replaced.

From the front windows on can look out upon the site of a tide mill at Kennedy's Lagoon, where the island's first grain was ground.

The Granville O. Haller residence in Coupeville may date back to 1866, believes Stanley Willhaight, its present owner, who has done considerable research on the subject. Major Haller, a veteran of the Indian War and first commandant at Fort Townsend, took a land claim at Crescent Harbor, but moved into town and became Coupeville's postmaster in 1867. He built a general merchandise store and warehouse on the waterfront across the street from his home.

The Works Progress Administration, in a study of early Washington architecture, cited this house as one of the best designed. It is a distinctly New England (Massachusetts) type, with central stack and arches in the bricks of the chimney. (The Rothschild house in Port Townsend has a similar chimney.) Downstairs are two identical fireplaces, back to back, and measuring about four feet in the width of the opening.

The main entrance hall has no stairway; the flight of steps faces another outside door between the dining room and small sitting room.

Haller moved to Seattle and later built a mansion on Minor Avenue, which stood until 1942. He sold his Coupeville house to D. O. Pearson, whose three daughters traveled west in company with one of the groups of "Mercer girls." After the Pearsons left there were several other owners and tenants. A fire occurred in the parlor side of the dwelling and water, used in extinguishing it, damaged other parts of the house. It had stood empty for 10 years when

Willhaight bought it in 1952 with the intention of gradually restoring the structure. In the course of making repairs he found that the walls are of 16-inch studding, with wide rough boards nailed diagonally on the outside. These are covered with clapboards, actually one-inch lumber laid on edge. They are as long as the full width of the house. Wrought square iron nails were used throughout. The shake roof was put on with the same square nails. The house was lathed and plastered, the lime being derived from shells on the beach. The lumber was from the mill at Utsalady.

Willhaight believes a ship carpenter must have done some of the finishing because brass knobs and latches in upstairs rooms are ship's hardware.

"The house probably has suffered more from abuse than age," Willhaight said.

It formerly had Grecian pillars on the porch and proper bannisters, as shown in an old picture. The interesting small bay windows once overlooked a beautiful garden with ponds.

The Libbey house in Coupeville was built by John Alexander, Jr., who lived at Mrs. Robert Fay's until it was completed in 1871. He sold the residence to Joseph Barstow Libbey, grandfather of the present occupant, Calvin Libbey.

This dwelling at Fifth and Main Streets has three Gothic arched bedroom windows on the second floor. One is a door that in years past opened on a small porch above the entrance. The porch has been removed and the main doorway with glass side panels shows to advantage. There were once ornamental boards on the gable ends. A quaint fireplace is still to be seen inside the house and old-style kitchen cupboards.

Alterations have not radically injured the lines of this dwelling, one of the very oldest on Whidbey Island. The kitchen wing was added at a later date.

Mrs. Willard Parker's residence at Third and Main Streets, Coupeville was designed by Howard Lovejoy in 1886 for John and Jane Kineth when they left their farm and went into town to live and enjoy closer association with neighbors. The ladies of the family are remembered as deriving much pleasure from sitting in their parlor with friends.

The house (page 54) was elegant by contemporary standards. Its entrance hall has a large newel post at the foot of the stairs, inlaid with panels of curly maple and mahogany. The parlor fireplace is of steel, painted to imitate red and black marble, with a scene in the center panel and smaller ones at the sides. Another unusual fireplace, with columns on either side, is in the dining rom. Ceilings of both rooms are centered with carved plaster medalions from which depended ornamental kerosene hanging lamps.

Originally the parlor woodwork was finished in black and silver.

The dining room has a large storage cupboard. A summer kitchen and woodshed were attached to the rear of the house, now used only for wood storage.

In the foreground (page 54 lower) is the Coupeville House owned by Miss J. J. Cook. It was erected about 1884 by Howard Lovejoy, one of Whidbey Island's outstanding builders. Interesting characteristics are the bay window with diagonal board trims, the mansard roof with the original shingles, the ornamental molding around the top of the walls and the detailed trim over all of the windows. The front door has four panels. One of the upstairs bed rooms has a view in three directions.

The house has remained in remarkably good condition. It stands on part of the old Captain Coupe land claim.

There is a question as to whether this home or the one beyond it was put up first and which was intended for Mrs. Lovejoy's mother. The Cook house appears to be the older. Mrs. Shirley Parker lives in the house next door, also built and formerly owned by Howard Lovejoy. The living room has a bay window extending to the second floor and forming the base of a cupalo on the roof. Fancy-butt shingles and the trim around the edge of the roof show Lovejoy's careful attention to details.

The original entrance hall and stairs with balusters and polished rail are unchanged, but the front porch was altered and converted into a sun porch. The pantry with its pitcher pump and cupboards became the sun room. Mrs. Parker said when she moved in nearly 50 years ago there was a zinc bath tub in the kitchen with a board cover on top. Only cistern water was available and the Parkers sprinkled their hedge from the cistern at the old court house, then across the street.

This residence, three quarters of a mile south of Prairie Center, was built in 1891 by Samuel Hancock, one of the earliest settlers on Whidbey Island. It was later bought by his brother Ernest, whose descendants still occupy the place. The back part was damaged by fire some years ago, so the kitchen was rebuilt, but in general the rest is little changed. The house has a distinctive crossed lattice trim and a bull's-eye attic window set in a gable end faced with fancy-cut shingles.

At the left side is a large bay-windowed room of a style appearing in several other island houses of the same period. It must have been taken from a pattern book and adapted by a building contractor to a dining room here, a livng room there, always allowing a bed chamber above and a turret shape to the roof.

Old residents recall that one formerly could see from this house an older Ernest Hancock residence far across the fields to the west. Now only the venerable barn remains.

Once the showplace of North Whidbey Island, the L. P. Byrne house still stands at the corner of Midway and 30th avenue E., near Oak Park. It was erected in 1894 by an Oak Harbor merchant and hotel owner.

Arches at the side of the bay windows gave the house distinction. The panes in an upstairs front bed room have been modernized; formerly they exactly matched the two windows below. An outside weather sheathing over the old clapboards fortunately has not altered the house too much. The front gables originally were crossed above the windows with a horizontal timber topped with an ornamental V. One of the four bed rooms was very large, with an alcove.

In its heyday the house boasted a windmill and a picket fence.

Out of Oak Harbor, at the junction of the Zylstra and Swantown roads is this house, built in 1911 by Benjamin Loers, who moved to Whidbey Island in 1896. He was a farmer and on his retirement put up the house. It was designed by William D. Rotschafer, a Netherlander who had built one like it in Holland, Mich. on the campus of Northwestern Theological Seminary.

The shingles on the dome were cut by hand from a piece of roofing. The windows in the tower have rounded wooden sashes and bowed glass.

The Loers family lived in the house until his death in 1939, then the heirs sold it to Mr. and Mrs. Vince Stroops, who have been there ever since.

Stroops is proud of the fact that, working alone, he renewed the shingles on the cupalo.

Fort Casey, on Whidbey Island, one of the triangle of forts defending the entrance to Puget Sound, was completed in 1906 and these were the officers' quarters. The single large house was the commandant's. They were declared Army surplus and now are used for summer educational activities.

The three forts—Casey, Worden and Flagler, were conceived as part of a coastal defense system when there was a threat of war with Spain. They served as military training centers during the First and Second World Wars, but never fired a shot except for maneuvers. The concept of defense changed several years after Fort Casey was completed and the armament had to be greatly altered.

Military posts such as Casey had a gay social life early in the century, with balls and parties and guests invited from a distance.

A retired sergeant in charge of the reservation when it was on caretaker status told of living in one of the large homes and how many buttons it was equipped with for summoning servants.

"We didn't have any," he said, "so our buzzes only called a member of the family."

Steilacoom

When Philip Keach built a handsome home on the waterfront at Steilacoom in 1858 for his bride, Antoinette Martin, he was already a leading business man of the town. The new Mrs. Keach was the daughter of Abner Martin, proprietor of the hotel in Steilacoom City, the rival townsite occupying the southern half of the present-day community.

Keach was a grocer, trail contractor, treasurer of Pierce County and an incorporator of the Puget Sound and Columbia River Railroad Co. He moved away from Steilacoom in the 1870's and the home was rented during the next decade until it was purchased by Henry Rupe, a brewer who thoroughly restored it. It is now owned by the C. V. Davidsons.

This residence was considered such a good example of pioneer architecture it was listed by the Works Progress Administration as worthy of preservation. A survey showed its outside walls and all partitions are of planks extending from the ground to the peak of the slate roof. It has four fireplaces with two double chimneys. The original cedar block foundation was replaced in 1955 with cement. Many of the window panes—12 to a window and eight to the five French doors—are of the early-day glass, which magnifies in spots and is otherwise imperfect. The muntin bars (divisions between panes) are very thin. The front door has four vertical and one horizontal panel.

Among the furnishings is the cradle owned by the Keach family and made by Nathaniel Orr, a Steilacoom cabinetmaker. Orr bought it back after the three Keach children had used it. He also acquired some of the family's cane-seated chairs. A descendant gave these pieces to the later owners of the house, so they are still there. The residence has had only four owners in the course of a century.

This is known as the Jesse Dunlap house. It is one of the oldest in Steilacoom and apparently dates from the 1850's. It has the original windows, typical large square chimney and overhanging roof.

The dwelling, at the corner of Pacific and Lafayette Streets, is slated for demolition soon, as it is no longer practical to maintain.

The view shown here is from the rear, the house having been altered on the street side to make space for a real estate office. The changes spoiled the good lines, as can be seen from the portion extending at the extreme right.

It is not clear who built the house. Early owners of the property were Lafayette Balch, who platted this portion of the town, and Oliver Meeker, who seems to have been an early purchaser. By 1862 it was in Mrs. Dunlap's name. Her husband was a teacher. They sold the property in 1873. Since 1888 it has been in the family of John L. Rigney, who came west in 1849 on the U.S.S. *Massachusetts*. He was among the first soldiers stationed at Fort Steilacoom. His wife accompanied him, she and another enlisted man's spouse being employed as laundresses for the military. Rigney took a 320-acre donation claim on Rigney Hill near Tacoma.

Descendants of the Rigneys remember when the house had a porch across the front with filagree trim. There were green window shutters, a cherry tree in the front yard and a large extension on the kitchen. The aunt who lived longest in the home married late in life to William O'Donnell, who was responsible for the alterations.

The Nathaniel H. Orr residence, dating approximately from 1857, stands on Rainier Street between Main and Balch in Steilacoom. The view on page 60 is of the south side. Owing to a screen of shrubbery it is difficult to photograph the building. The front door, hidden by the trees to the right, has window-lights on three sides as shown in the lower picture. The roof ends are finished with returned cornices.

The shed roof in the foreground is over the kitchen, which was remodelled inside to allow space for a bath. The corner toward the street formerly was open and intended for storage of wood. One can see the joining where boards were added to create a room.

Almost nothing about the house has been changed throughout the years except for slight modernization. Windows and chimneys are as they were when Orr married Emma Thompson in 1869 and brought his bride from Victoria to live in the building where he had his carpenter shop. The dwelling never had a front porch. Its first staircase was outside on the north face of the building. Later Orr finished a highly polished, oak-railed flight of stairs inside. He moved his business to another structure in his large yard and the shop became a living room. The Orrs needed space, as they had eight children.

The home has been owned continuously in the same family, therefore it has been excellently preserved, with respect for tradition. It contains many furnishings brought by the original occupants from Victoria. Orr, a Virginian, was a wagonmaker and

woodworker. He put excellent craftsmanship into his house. Nothing is out of plumb in it to this day. Glenn Orr, his grandson, the present owner, can point to wooden pegs and square nails in the walls, driven by his grandfather.

Steilacoom once had two brickyards, one producing good bricks, the other making a kind that crumbled. Grandfather Orr knew the good quality when he saw them and the brick work in his house never had to be replaced.

When dormer windows were added to Miles West's old home in Steilacoom, it was found the house was of log construction, covered with clapboards.

West lived in Steilacoom as early as 1858, but did not remain long, selling his house on Puyallup Street, between Lafayette and Rainier, to Peter Runquest, blacksmith. The latter arrived at Fort Vancouver in 1849 and was sent with the troops to Fort Steilacoom. When he took up his new residence he opened a blacksmith shop farther up the hill in the next block. The structure was later made over into a dwelling.

After a time he decided it was too windy living

on the hill, so he erected another home on lower, less exposed ground. His first dwelling is heavily shaded with trees. Perhaps some are from the seeds he brought west from Kentucky to shade him in his old age.

The West house is one of the few in town with remains of a picket fence, protection in the days when cows ran loose.

This is the rear entrance to the Albert Balch house, set in an attractive garden in Steilacoom. The home dates from late in the 1850's. Formerly it was entirely of clapboards; the upper section was shingled by a later occupant. As a consequence of having to move the house back from the street, the fireplaces were damaged and no longer exist. At present the front has bargeboards, but these are an addition; the old house was beautifully simple, with overhanging eaves and front windows almost from floor to ceiling. The early-day front door with side and top-lights is still there.

Albert Balch was the brother of Lafayette Balch, town founder, who built this residence for him. Al-

bert was in Steilacoom as early as 1856, for he was named on the jury that tried Chief Leschi for murder. The 1860 census lists Albert as single, aged 35, a merchant from Maine. It is said that he became ill and returned to his home state. As a consequence, when Lafayette died suddenly in 1862 no one of the family remained at Steilacoom to perpetuate the name.

Lafayette Balch, a sea captain and owner of the brig *George Emery,* first did business selling piles, cordwood, fish and hides from around Puget Sound. When he decided to make Steilacoom his headquarters he unloaded lumber for a building and set up a store in it. Then he platted a townsite on 320 acres he staked, despite being unable to get title to them while the Hudson's Bay Co. still claimed the land. The patent was issued 16 years after his death, during which period the property had changed hands various times.

Balch attracted settlers to his town by donating land for public enterprises such as a court house, church and school. He had expected to marry and was building a new home for his prospective bride when he went to San Francisco to fetch her. Instead he dropped dead on a street in the Bay City. His intended honeymoon house stood until about 1935.

This home of Captain Bartlett on Stevens Street at Sixth, in Steilacoom, is more interesting than appears at first glance. It was erected in the 1860's and originally had a roof line with filagree bargeboards, a portion of which can be seen in the picture.

In 1907 Dr. Charles McCutcheon purchased the house and raised the roof in front so as to have more overhead space in the bed rooms. Another room was added toward the street.

Least changed is the dining room, with its original fireplace and interesting stair. It looks upon a porch and through the windows one has a magnificent view of Puget Sound.

The picket fence has been kept in excellent repair and has been there a long time. The present owners are interested in preserving the atmosphere of the house and have done everything possible to restore it. A recent addition was a paneled front door acquired from another house of the 1860's in the process of demolition.

Captain George W. Black, a native of Nova Scotia, built this house in Steilacoom. He was a bachelor sea captain, who came west about 1864. He died in 1892, aged 62.

This rear view of his house is more interesting than the front because of the lacework and the rarely-encountered windows on the stair landing.

This is a Gothic type cottage with gingerbread bargeboards on all sides. Formerly the porch extended entirely across the front.

The house now is roofed with plastic shingles. Since an earthquake damaged the chimneys they are enclosed in cement. The garage (at left of the photo) was the former laundry and wood shed. There is a modern front door, but the top and side-lights are as they were.

In 1889 the house was purchased by Mrs. Dorothea Claussen, who remodeled it. Prior to that the stairs were not enclosed with a door, as at present.

The yard has very old maple trees and a California pine.

The Jim Hughes house at Rainier and Main Streets, Steilacoom dates from 1890. The wing to the left was added later and contains a large chimney. The main part of the white house used to have a porch across the front. E. J. Sheley is the present occupant. The red cottage next door was also built by the Hughes family.

These are excellent examples of starkly simple utilitarian architecture when what was useful counted more than imaginative touches. Cottages similar to Hughes' sprang up by the hundreds in Washington communities, especially in mill and mining towns.

This is a side view of Waverly, a 17-room mansion at the corner of Commercial and Wilkes Streets, Steilacoom, built in 1891 by E. R. Rogers, pioneer merchant. He opened the McCaw and Rogers store in 1859.

Next door to the mansion is one of the oldest houses in town which had belonged to Captain Webster. After his death Mrs. Webster married Rogers. She had a daughter by her first marriage and when the large house was built Rogers arranged an apartment for the young woman across the front of the second floor.

The family did not long enjoy their new home, for there were delays in construction, then when it was finished the panic of 1893 wiped out the owner's title on a mortgage.

Shortly after that Mr. and Mrs. Charles Herman of Walla Walla moved in and she kept summer boarders, as her husband was in poor health. It was Mrs. Herman who gave the house its name, for the brand of bicycle she liked to ride.

From then on the house had lodgers much of the time, railroad workers, paper-mill employees and soldiers' families. After the Second World War it stood empty and deteriorated. Vandals tore out fixtures and sawed some of the woodwork. The place had been a "haunted house" when, in 1960, Clarence Dowling began renovating it and again rented rooms.

Instead of clothes closets the house had large dressing rooms. When new it had only two baths, one each on the first and second floors. There was a wood stove in every room except the attic, where five rooms are sealed with beaded wainscoting. One of these chambers across the front of the third floor apparently was a party room.

A curiosity is the transoms over all doors. The dining room formerly had a bell board to show calls coming from elsewhere in the big house.

Another feature is the double parlor. Between the hall and the front parlor was elaborate wooden grillework, of which a few traces remain. The interior trim was largely Douglas fir paneling finished in two tones. The house had many room-size bay windows and an unobstructed view of Puget Sound.

Mrs. Rogers is said to have planted the two large honey locust trees in the front yard.

Olympia Area

Here is a farmhouse from pre-Indian War times. It stands on the Yelm Road southeast of Olympia on the Captain Gilmore Hays donation claim. He had migrated west in 1852 in the same wagon train as B. F. Yantis and his family. Both men lost their wives in Idaho and were left with motherless children.

Hays' eldest daughter, Jerusha, had to take over the duties of housekeeper. It was at this place that she was courted by the pioneer steamboat man, Captain John G. Parker.

"There were no wagon roads then," she related, "only rough trails and all women rode horseback-sidesaddle. We sewed our own dresses by hand, crocheted our own lace trimmings. There were only four of us girls of marriageable age just then and we were very popular; we rode our horses to many dances."

Hays in 1854 became restless to visit Missouri again and in order to get away rushed his daughter into marriage. "Parker wants you and I want to go East," was his argument.

Parker arrived to escort Jerusha for a visit to a Bush Prairie home and when she wasn't ready, asked why. She said, "You'd better ask father.'

Hays put it to the young man that, since both young people were apparently considering marriage, they'd better get it over with. Parker was convinced easily. He returned to town, found Chief Justice Lander and Yantis and brought them both out. Sarah Yantis was already there as another witness. A young man who was clearing land for Hays cooked the wedding supper, consisting of ham, hot biscuits and sauce made of dried fruits.

Hays made his journey east and returned in time to play a prominent role in the Indian War.

The farm where the rush wedding took place was long owned by P. Wickie and is now the property of the Olympia Brewing Co.

Most often referred to as the Senator A. S. Ruth house, this one is on the southeast corner of Capital Way and Maple Park in Olympia. The view from the front does not reflect its great age because the porch and fancy shingles were added later. The door, however, is in the older style.

Senator Ruth, a civil engineer from Maine, moved to Thurston County in 1892 and served in the legislature from 1901 to 1911.

The house previously was the home of Captain and Mrs. J. J. Gilbert and was built for them by the wife's father, Judge B. F. Yantis, who came West in the early 1850's from Missouri. Mrs. Gilbert (Frances Yantis) at the age of 3 lost her mother when the wagon train reached Idaho.

This is one of Olympia's oldest residences still occupied.

Four generations of the same family have occupied the dwelling at 918 E. Glass Street, Olympia, built by Daniel Richardson Bigelow, pioneer lawyer and member of the first legislature.

He was born in Belleville, N.Y. in 1824, crossed the plains by wagon train in 1850 to Portland and sailed in the schooner *Exact* for Puget Sound the following year. Olympia then was comprised of a dozen frame cabins of primitive architecture, covered with split cedar siding and described as "well ventilated, but healthy." The only two-story building was the Michael Simmons store and post office, with the customs house upstairs. A short distance from the village were two dozen Indian huts.

Bigelow settled on a 320-acre land claim in 1853. He had opened a law office, was elected treasurer of newly-created Thurston County and was made code commissioner to prepare laws for Washington Territory. He served as Olympia's school superintendent and was sent to the legislature in 1854, drawing a three-year term in the upper house. He also became justice of the peace.

That same year he married Elizabeth White and in the summer commenced construction of the house that has survived considerably more than a century.

Daniel and Elizabeth had eight children. He died in 1905.

Now another Daniel Bigelow, a grandson, and his wife and four sons live in the old home. Many of the original furnishings are in it, including the first Bigelow's desk and law books. Other items are cherry wood dining chairs, a reed organ, square piano and various pieces brought by sailing ships in the early days.

The house is Gothic revival style, with two and a half floors and 10½ foot ceilings. It has undergone many changes, some of the ceilings being lowered and the seven original rooms divided so that there are now 14. Remodelling has had curious effects and in one place a former stairway leads nowhere. Some rooms do not have windows of equal size or distance from the floor. The exterior has been altered by removal of the covered porches across the front of the right wing and the central portion. Of

the seven original fireplaces three remain. All are small, intended to burn Washington coal. The tall main double chimney has been replaced by another of different design.

Despite these changes, some of the old window glass and plaster are still to be seen. The gardens are gone and the land is reduced in size to half a city block, enclosed by a black iron fence. While the stables and woodshed stand, the carriage house was torn down and its timbers used for another structure.

Long ago the Bigelow home was on the outskirts of Olympia and reached only by water; today the city surrounds it.

This was once a conspicuous landmark on the lonely road from Cowlitz Landing to Olympia. It was built in 1878 by William Owen Bush, eldest son of George Bush, both members of the first American colony on Puget Sound. Owen, as he was called, was 12 years old when he journeyed west by wagon with his parents in the party led by Michael Simmons in 1845.

George Bush and his wife, Isabelle, had a 640-acre donation claim on Bush Prairie and lived southeast of the present Olympia airport. They are said to have started with a log cabin, then moved into a split-cedar home and finally into a house of sawed boards, with glass windows, an upstairs and rooms lined with wall paper. Here George Bush died in 1863 and three sons inherited the home-

stead. Owen up to the time of his father's death had been on a farm he bought on Mound Prairie. Now he moved back to the paternal acres and designed a two-story house with bay windows and two fire-places. Mr. Barnes, a carpenter, built it for him. Two others were erected afterward in the same enclosed yard, one for John S. Bush and the other for his in-laws, Mr. and Mrs. George Gaston.

Owen's house stood on the site of his father's first log cabin and was surrounded with gardens and fruit trees. The Bushes were all celebrated for their hospitality and for their skill as horticulturists. Owen won a national medal for cereals he exhibited at the Philadelphia exposition in 1876.

He became head of the family ranch and carried on its operation for 40 years. The place is remembered for its stake-and-rider fence, picket-enclosed yard, swept clean and packed hard, and its flowers planted along the rows of vegetables.

After the harvest time the granary (which had been George Bush'es last home) was cleared for a celebration and dancing. At Christmas and Thanksgiving Owen's house was the scene of family dinners with maybe 25 sitting down to the table.

It is said that in a division of property, probably after Owen's death in 1906, his house was lifted on four wagons and moved a quarter of a mile from its hilltop site to a prairie close to the river.

Not much remains but memories of the hospitable home travelers could see a long distance away. It is open to the weather now, the haunt of barnyard animals. Both it and the old John S. Bush house, shown here, have been given to the Soroptomist Club at Olympia, which will take steps toward their preservation.

At the corner of Tenth and Adams Streets in Olympia are two very old structures, once part of an academy, but now converted into residences. The smaller of the two was a wing of the building, which was divided when moved. The larger contains several apartments.

Olympia had a Puget Sound Wesleyan Institute as early as 1856, but it does not appear to have owned a building and in 1861 it was closed out at a sheriff's sale. Another school followed, the Union Academy, which in 1883 was reorganized as the Olympia Collegiate Institute, under supervision of the Methodist Episcopal conference. At one time, after the institute closed, the building served as the old Central School.

In 1890, when 200 students were attending the Collegiate Institute, an announcement stated that all applicants would be admitted "who are willing to work." It added: "Testimonials of good moral character are required of applicants unknown to the principal. Students coming from other institutions of learning must furnish certificates of honorable dismissal. The rules of the institution are few in number, and are designed to promote self-reliance and true nobility of character."

This well-preserved home at 1010 Franklin Street, Olympia once belonged to Dr. Alden Hatch Steele, who started for Oregon in 1849 and for 14 years practiced medicine at Oregon City. While there he was 11 years a member of the city council and three years mayor. He married Miss Hannah Blackler in 1854. He was later appointed post surgeon at Fort Dalles and then was transferred to Fort Stevens and in 1868 to Fort Steilacoom. When the fort was abandoned a year later he declined further Army service, moved to Olympia and built his home soon afterward.

He successively held other public posts such as physician to the Nisqually and Chehalis Indian reservations, examining surgeon for Army and Navy pensions and, from 1876 to 1880, regent of the Territorial University. He was medical inspector for the Territorial Penitentiary and for 25 years medical examiner for a life insurance company. He was also a director of the First National Bank of Olympia, helped organize gas and power companies and was interested in the Olympia Hotel. He died in 1902.

Tumwater, the oldest American community on Puget Sound, has one of the most venerable houses in the state. Though not erected by founders of the town, it followed closely after them and is a splendid example of the earliest frame construction. The builder, young Nathaniel Crosby III, had ample resources to draw upon, among them his family's sawmill for basic material and a ship for bringing luxury items.

In 1849 Michael Simmons, who led the first American party to the Sound sold the grist mill and sawmill he had operated at Tumwater to the firm of Crosby and Gray of Oregon City. Capt. Nathaniel Crosby II had come to the Coast in 1844 and, after his new investment, purchased the brig *Grecian* and brought his family from Massachusetts. He and his brother, Clanrick, took up residence at Tumwater. Nathaniel spent his time at sea, but Clanrick opened a general store and erected a larger flour mill.

Nathaniel II died at Hong Kong. His son married Cordelia Jane Smith and purchased a piece of his uncle's land for a home site overlooking the head of Puget Sound. The bride and groom erected the house about 1854. It had a parlor, dining room, kitchen, storeroom and immense woodshed. A stairway in the entrance hall led up to four bed rooms. One of the notable features is a stair rail made of a straight branch of a yew tree, polished to satin smoothness.

Nat and Cordelia were the grandparents of singer Bing (Harry) Crosby, who was born in Tacoma and who in the 1940's contributed generously to a fund for saving the old house. It had changed owners numerous times and was threatened with destruction. It now stands in the midst of a freeway complex and is visible from Highway U.S. 5. To inspect it more closely one must drive into the town of Tumwater.

The cherry trees still in the yard were planted by Nathaniel Crosby III.

This abandoned home at 317 Eighth Avenue, Olympia belonged to Dr. Nathaniel Ostrander and here he and his wife raised their large family. The house was built after they moved from Tumwater in 1879 and stood alone on the block for a time. It is distinguished by the gable over the entrance porch, the second-floor arched door and a front door with glass lights above and at the sides.

Dr. Ostrander was a prominent pioneer, for whom the town of Ostrander is named. He was born in Ulster County, N.Y. and was sent to an uncle in New York City to be educated until he was 14. As a young man he went to the Middle West, clerked in a store and married. He began studying medicine while farming. He was graduated from St. Louis University in 1848 and practiced medicine two years before joining the westward immigration to California, where he continued his practice in mining camps.

After several more years he returned to the Midwest, sold his farm and joined his father in a wagon train. The ultimate destination was the Cowlitz Valley, where the physician again farmed and practiced medicine. In 1872 he moved to Tumwater and opened a drug store. His last move was to Olympia, where he lived until his death in 1902 at the age of 84.

Dr. Ostrander was the first probate judge in Cowlitz County, serving 12 years. He was a member of the legislature for one term, was twice mayor of Olympia and several times on its city council.

Here lived Judge O. B. McFadden after he moved from Chehalis to Olympia. He spent all of the latter part of his life in this house at 916 Adams Street and died here in 1875. Frank P. McFadden, civil engineer, stayed on in the family home.

Bay windows have remained as they were, but some alteration has taken place in the front porch, which must have once been similar to that of Dr. Ostrander's home.

At 1104 Franklin Street, Olympia is this house which has been the abode of several state officials in the past. It was for a long time associated with the Bush Baker family.

Although from this view the appearance is of a small cottage, there are sizeable additions in the rear. The bargeboards and bay windows go back to the 1890's.

This large dwelling at 1431 Eleventh Avenue E., Olympia was erected about 1890 by William G. White. It has had many owners and is now occupied by Mr. and Mrs. W. M. McBee, who have endeavored to furnish it in true Victorian style.

The square tower, jigsaw work, turned posts, turned bars and unique bargeboards in the gables draw much attention to the home, especially as it stands on a slight knoll amid well-kept grounds.

77

Another of the oldest remaining houses in Olympia is at 1239 Eighth Avenue and was built by Mr. Patnude. It is extremely interesting for its moldings under the neatly boxed eaves. These scallops adorn all of the gables and are carried out in a smaller pattern around the edge of the porch roof. The brackets on the porch columns are exceptional, with their scalloped edge joined to the molding in a continuous design. Two arched windows upstairs in front are other Gothic touches.

Now a half-way house for convalescent alcoholics, this home high above West Bay Drive in Olympia was built in the 1890's by an early mayor, George B. Lane, who had been a college professor.

From 1910 to 1933 the residence was owned by the Helenius family, then it became a boarding house until its present use.

Gingerbread bargeboards, spindle trims, porches and bay windows were employed liberally by the original builder. Almost every room has a view from its windows.

Once among Olympia's show places, this house at 826 East 8th Street was unoccupied when photographed. It was erected by Coridon Z. Mason, proprietor of the Olympia Iron Works. He had trained as an architect and probably his taste greatly influenced the design. A study of the exterior reveals many cutwork gimmicks at the height of their popularity early in the 1890's, such as spindles, fancy-butt shingles, brackets, window-glass borders and several types of scroll trims for the gables.

The executive mansion in Olympia, a red brick veneer on a knoll west of the Capitol, was completed in the winter of 1908-9. Governor Samuel G. Cosgrove, who was to have been its first occupant, was critically ill on his inauguration day. He went to California instead of moving in and died in the South two months later.

Although the mansion had not yet been lived in, two official housewarmings were held in it, one for the legislators and the other for the public at large. Legislators were the first to dance in the ball room and the first to be served from the kitchen. Visitors on this festive occasion had an opportunity to inspect the 17 rooms. Planners had visualized the west side as the private home of the governor and the east side as the public portion for social functions and official guests. Specifications called for a small office and a large reception hall for the governor on the second floor. Some of the items included by the architect were a wine cooler, pastry pantry, pot closet, trunk room, trunk lift running from basement to garret, billiard room, burglar-and-fireproof vault, vegetable room, wine room and fuel room.

There was pressure on the State Building Commission to have the residence constructed entirely of Washington materials. Somehow Alaskan marble

keystones went in over the windows and door casings, though the rest of the exterior trim was Wilkeson sandstone.

As a consequence of Cosgrove's death, Lieutenant Governor Marion E. Hay of Spokane became the first occupant of the stately Georgian house.

In 1933, under Governor Clarence B. Martin, some remodelling was done to bring the place up to date and make it more cheerful. At that time the brick fireplace in the drawing room was faced with pink marble. Wall-to-wall carpet was laid over the oak floors and the second floor was changed and a bar and kitchenette installed there. Governor Albert Rosellini during his term added other luxury items, including hand-wrought candelabra for the drawing room mantel.

The governors have not always been pleased with their house, which was not weatherstripped until Governor Rosellini's administration. Some of the early occupants rebelled over the early-type electrical installations dating from the time when 25-watt tungsten lamps on a cord drop were considered brilliant illumination. Of course, improvements have been made and are still going on.

Port Townsend Area

To A. Horace Tucker belongs credit for many of Port Townsend's best vintage houses. His own classic dwelling was constructed in 1867 for his bride. In 1865 he built the first church, St. Paul's Episcopal, and he and his wife, Jane Caines, were the initial couple married in it, August 27, 1867. It is said that a crowd was on hand to give them a charivari, but they slipped away and took a honeymoon trip to Sequim on the plunger *Kate Alexander*. The voyage was rough and Jane was desperately sick. Tucker had to leave his spouse with friends and returned in a canoe piloted by an Indian and his squaw.

Tucker was born in Portsmouth, N.H. in 1839 and lived to the great old age of 99. His father had come around Cape Horn in 1849 and went from California to the Fraser River gold rush in 1858. Horace made his first ocean voyage at 15. He journeyed west in 1862 by way of the Isthmus of Panama and joined his father, John Tucker, in Port Townsend. The young man brought a collection of house plans which aided him in his carpentering career.

In early days he was Port Townsend's coffin maker. He held many town offices and was mayor. In 1890 he erected a three-story building at Water and Adams Streets of bricks produced at his Point Wilson brickyard. He and his partner, Brooks, had the contract to build the flight of stairs up the Taylor Street hill in 1875.

Tucker lived in his well-built home the rest of his life and his son continued to occupy it. Then the Daubenburger family owned it briefly, but decided they needed more space and sold to the Worfords. Many Tucker belongings were in the house when the Daubenburgers moved in and they still have a few pieces. The attic contained old trunks and Mrs. Daubenburger searched them in vain, hoping to find the famous house-plan books Horace Tucker had brought with him as a young man.

Here, at Polk and Washington Streets in Port Townsend, lived Captain Enoch S. Fowler, who was in and out of the harbor on some of the earliest vessels on Puget Sound. He was from Lubec, Maine and had come West to the California gold rush. He paid his first visit to the Sound in 1852, retired from the sea in 1857 and married the widow of another sea captain.

Fowler built Port Townsend's first dock at which a vessel could land safely; he constructed the stone building now occupied by The Leader, the oldest business structure in town (1874), and promoted many other local enterprises until his death in 1876.

Early in 1854 he purchased the schooner *R. B. Potter* and chartered her to Governor Stevens as a mail and dispatch boat. After its release from territorial service he operated it as the first regular mail packet on the route between Olympia, Seattle, Port Townsend and Victoria.

His is the oldest frame dwelling in Port Townsend. Mrs. A. B. Barrie, who has lived in it since the early 1920's, has remodelled the interior. When she did so she found that the foundation under the back portion still had bark on the old timbers. This extension was a summer kitchen with a large pantry. Beneath the kitchen was a cistern. As the house settled, the rim came up through the floor. In the course of probing around the foundation to make repairs, a large number of bottles were unearthed, still containing a beverage under Dutch seal.

The house was erected before 1865—how much earlier is not known, but it was still in the era of simple classic lines and returned cornices. The stairway was purely utilitarian in appearance, but there were decorative moldings in the living room and master's bed room and a built-in seat beside the solitary fireplace. One of the few concessions to ornament was a pull-down oil lamp with an etched bowl in the front hall.

The house still has some of the cloudy window panes of long ago.

On the Jefferson Street slope of the hill back of the business section of Port Townsend is one of that city's oldest mansions, maintained by the Washington Parks and Recreation Commission as a historical site. The dwelling was built by Tucker in 1868 for David C. H. Rothschild, prominent merchant. He moved to Port Townsend in 1858 and opened the Kentucky Store, which carried clothing, dry goods, boots and shoes, liquors, tobacco, cigars and Yankee notions. The owner advertised that he handled "cloths, cassimeres and vestings" and that suits could be made to order "by a practical tailor."

Rothschild conducted his mercantile business for 20 years before turning to shipping. He acted as agent for many lines until his death in 1886.

His first home was near the waterfront in quarters over his store. When he fixed upon a sightly location for his new dwelling he built well and it withstood a century of aging with dignity. Little work was required for its restoration by the Parks Department.

Long ago the house represented the height of elegance. The flowered parlor wall paper has a gold background and is topped by a series of borders, one of crimson velvet, edged with a narrow molding coated with gold leaf. Above it is a border of figured paper and a wider molding also of gold leaf.

Front windows upstairs reach to the floor and open on a porch with a view. Woodwork was grained by hand with a paint brush.

As the house remained continuously in the same family, some of the Rothschilds' wedding presents are among the furnishings. Every room contains some article of interest to the connoisseur. Old clothing is stored in the tall wardrobes, a kitchen cupboard holds dishes of rare old English patterns, the Florence sewing machine patented in 1850 still is in working order, the piano, shipped west in 1886, has a delightful tone. The cellar holds a fascinating array of screened food safes, bottle racks for wine storage, bird cages, grinders for sausage meat, an apple-corer, crocks and demijohns.

This is a near perfect example of a substantial early-day home with no extraneous objects brought in. The gardens and orchard have given way to space for parking visitors' cars and the barn and wash house that stood in the rear were removed because they were unsafe. Little else has been altered.

This residence at 633 Van Buren Street in Port Townsend was built by Captain James McIntyre on property he acquired in 1871 from F. W. Pettygrove, one of the town founders. His daughter, Sophia, married the captain and the house was erected between 1875 and 1880. It first consisted of an oblong floor plan with kitchen wing in back. The wing with the two-story bay windows was added several years later.

Captain McIntyre, at 70, was lost at sea when he went down with his ship, the collier *Bristol*, after it struck a rock on the Alaskan coast in 1902.

The McIntyres had a beautiful daughter, Lucy, whose name is worked into the painted grained woodwork on the door of her childhood room. Lucy married a surveyor, Mr. Hough, and they had two sons, Calvin and Charley, whose names adorn two cupboard doors in the house.

Two Port Townsendites, Max Levy and Ed Sims, were in Alaska at this time and married girls from the territory. Sims brought his wife to Port Townsend, where she was not accepted by local society. Levy accompanied them, but did not bring his wife. He and Lucy met and subsequently she divorced Hough and married Levy. He was a dapper little man of cosmopolitan tastes and his home was considered among the most elegant in town.

There was a canopy over the front walk from the front door to the street that was used for big parties, of which there are reported to have been many. The grounds were well kept and surrounded by a wrought iron fence three feet high. A great cedar of Lebanon tree stood at the corner of the property where is now a gazebo. The tree died in a freezing winter a few years before the present owners acquired the property. The gazebo with which they replaced it is from St. John's Hospital and was erected by the same carpenter who built the bandstand in Chetzemoka Park.

The carriage house was moved to the property by Captain McIntyre from a location near Washington Street. The Levys kept a black mare and drove her hitched to a smart single-seat gig. It is related that a servant would hitch up the mare, bring the gig around to the front gate and the Levys would emerge in fine attire and drive down to Water Street with little boys running after them in awe. The couple would drive out to the dock and often would board a ship for San Francisco, where they visited for long periods.

Max Levy was admired by some persons and disliked by others. He was identified with the more seamy aspects of the town, as were many other "respectable" citizens at that time when the place was a wide-open port and shanghaiing of sailors, bawdy houses and saloons were thriving businesses.

The house in 1939 went to Sophia Bliss, Mrs.

Levy's daughter. The house was never outside of the family except for three years prior to its purchse by Ralph Raphael, the present owner, seven years ago. No alterations have been made from its original state. Marble fireplaces and an impressive wood and glass mantelpiece are still intact. Additions made recently are in the same general style.

This is the oldest brick house in Port Townsend, built in 1878 by Hiram Parrish. It stands at 641 Calhoun Street. A later owner, R. E. Ammeter renovated the structure.

The brick was the product of John Stockand and Thomas Drummond, brothers-in-law who had a brickyard on the S. M. Eskildsen farm toward Discovery Bay. Drummond was a stone and brick mason, besides being a master mechanic.

The James DeLeo home at Taylor and Lawrence Streets, Port Townsend probably was built between 1876 and 1882 during the time when the property belonged to N. D. Hill. In those days he was a wholesale and retail pharmacist, a member of the city council and one of the town's leading citizens.

The house has an elaborate exterior, fancy-butt shingles, wrought iron railing, a rising sun on the front gable, spindles along the upper portion of the porch, elaborate posts and decor of the window frames.

The Frank Bartlett house at 314 Polk Street, Port Townsend, was built in 1883 and is one of the town's attractions. Bartlett was in the general merchandise business, did some stevedoring and was involved in financial transactions during the boom period. He was county treasurer and a town councilman. He was a son of Charles C. Bartlett, who owned the house across the street. Both homes are on the rim of the hill, with an excellent view.

The French provincial house (page 87) is notable for its mansard roof. It has fireplaces in parlor, library and dining room. The one in the living room is of marbleized pressed iron, imported from France. The library fireplace has Portuguese tiles and the one in the dining room has English tiles. The mantels are plain.

Ceilings are 12 feet 4 inches high and have medallions in the center. The front bay windows are alcoved, with arches above them. The hand rail on the stairs is rosewood.

The classic floor plan called for a central hall and a drawing room 32 feet long. The family did its living on the other side, where there was a library, bed room and morning room, attached to the kitchen. In recent years the morning room has been converted into a furnace room.

The drawing room was on the water side and behind it a 26-foot dining room. An open porch across this side later was enclosed in glass.

Mrs. Bartlett loved to entertain. A tradition of the house was that on New Year's Eve the gentlemen

present on the stroke of midnight went into the garden and dug up a jug, enjoyed its contents, filled and reburied it.

The house cost $10,000 to build, which was a large sum in those days. The property formerly spread over half a block. The place once sold for taxes for $2,500. When hard times hit Port Townsend the Bartletts suffered reverses and ran a boarding house.

The upstairs bed rooms are large. One is 26 feet long and had originally been a billiard room. The house was built before the age of indoor plumbing and bathing was done with water carried to dressing rooms.

In their affluent days the Bartletts kept Chinese servants. who lived over the carriage house.

The George W. Downs residence, 538 Filmore Street, Port Townsend, built in 1886, is now the home of Mayor Frank M. Smith. Downs was first identified with the sawmill at Port Discovery and moved to Port Townsend in 1881 to run another mill on Point Hudson, for which the townsfolk had formed a stock company.

The house has 11 foot 9 inch ceilings and four fireplaces. The carved wood mantelpiece in the living room, at present painted white, looks most attractive around the brown ceramic tile.

The blue, yellow and burgundy prism glass window, centered with a bird, beside the front entrance, was an addition after the house was built. In its original state a porch was where this now is, but Mrs. Downs thought the front door too close to the foot of the stairs, so the wall was removed, a two-story bay was added and the door was moved to one side. The little uncovered porch formerly above the entrance was closed in and became a sewing room.

A cupola and a widow's walk were other ornamental fancies, but when these became discolored from chimney smoke and a leak developed, the roof was altered and left flat on top. At the same time a filagree wooden fence over the side bay windows was taken down.

The stair rail and newel post are the originals, so are the wooden window shutters and hall light fixture.

This dwelling has not had many changes of occupants. Mr. Downs' sister, Mrs. Fox, lived there after he was gone. She sold to a family who stayed only a year, then it was in charge of a caretaker until Smith purchased it. The structure was kept in excellent condition. Among articles still in it were 200 old Harpers Magazines of the 1880's and 1890's. The Smiths noticed a cut place in the kitchen floor boards, lifted out the flooring and found a combination cistern and well under the house (in the back yard was another cistern). In the well were 175 bottles of all kinds, some tracing back to an early-day pharmacy.

The present owners happened to possess considerable Victorian furniture, most appropriate for the gracious old rooms.

A feature of the Francis Wilcox James house, opposite the post office in Port Townsend, is its chimney that disappears and reappears again. The mansion (upper, page 90) has some of the fanciest shingles in the state— three types of patterns. It belongs to W. A. Eaton, who has been converting it into a Victorian inn.

James, a native of England, arrived in Port Townsend in 1853 and became a customs inspector. In 1855 he went to LaPush and two years later was appointed lightkeeper at Cape Flattery. On his return to Port Townsend he managed a trading store, which he sold to C. C. Bartlett. James retired in 1882 and, as he had a shrewd head for finance, he devoted himself to his investments from then on. At the time of his death in 1920 he left one of the largest estates ever accumulated in Jefferson County.

James built his house about 1889 for his wife in New England, but she died before coming west. He lived alone there except for the housekeeper, whom he later married.

Inlaid hardwood parquet in the entrance hall and the master's suite were unusual in Port Townsend. The stairs are finished with wild cherrywood brought around Cape Horn from Virginia and carved locally in a spiral design on the newel post. The brickwork was laid of imported bricks, the work done by an English brickmason. There are five usable fireplaces and four others that have been sealed off.

Eaton has left the entire main floor as it was and made 12 bed rooms out of the rest of the house. Upstairs the whole front section on the right of the second floor was the master's suite, with dressing room and arched alcove for bay window and a sliding glass door leading to the captain's walk in front of it. James is said to have sat out there often in his overcoat, watching the ships in the harbor.

The house has filagree door knobs and hand-carved bronze hinges, but only a small amount of stained glass. All of the woodwork is finished with medallions clear to the third floor. Brick walls in the basement are 18 inches thick and there are places in the house where Eaton, engaged in re-wiring, had to drill through 36 inches of wall. Refinishing is hard on electric tools, he said, and dulls them quickly.

The carriage house was once taller than the residence, having a tank on top that furnished water to part of the town. James had an artesian well on his property.

This old dwelling had one risque chapter in its history when it was leased by a doctor for a hospital. The law lowered the boom on it and and closed the establishment because of abortions the physician was alleged to have performed.

Port Townsend's noblest example of "carpenters' Gothic" is the George E. Starrett house, erected in 1889 and bearing the name of the House of the Four Seasons from a series of murals inside its domed entrance.

Starrett, a leading contractor and builder, was for a time operator of the sawmill at Point Hudson and principal supplier of the town's lumber. He ran the mill until it expired of sheer decrepitude. A kindly man, he gave employment to many old derelicts.

Starrett, a native of Maine, arrived in Port Townsend in 1885 and two years later married Ann Van Bokkelen, daughter of a prominent pioneer. Starrett contracted to build the first Catholic Church, he dabbled in real estate, organized the Port Townsend Dry Dock Co. in 1892 and was interested in the nail company.

His house was fascinating both inside and out. Originally the tower was topped with a weathervane. Below this were eight little gables and under and behind them the dome with triangular painted panels of the seasons by an artist named Chapman, who also did the frescoes in the Presbyterian Church. The scantily draped figure of Winter shocked some of the townsfolk, who severely criticized the Starretts for permitting a "lewd" painting in their home.

Frescoes adorned the lower walls in the entrance hall and traces can still be detected, though they have long since been given an over-coating.

Ceilings are 12 feet and no door molding went without a special motif for corner medallions in the principal rooms—lions in the hall, a dove in one room, a fern in another, a geometric pattern in another. Frescoes of fruit adorned the dining room and flowers are on the music room walls.

While the paintings have attracted much attention, little mention has been made of the variety of exterior trim on the mansion. No gable went without carpentry adornment, some more elaborate than others, such as a star, a sunrise, wing-like scrolls and a heraldic design resembling a harp.

The staircase in the entrance hall is a free-hung spiral with two complete turns. Bannisters and newel posts were carved in five kinds of wood. The third floor windows in the tower, together with the railing, form an indoor widow's walk.

The brass candle light fixture which formerly topped the newel post now graces a table in the house. George Nichols, who owns the home, was able to acquire a bed and settee which had been the Starretts'. Before Nichols bought the place it had been divided into apartments. He has since restored it as much as possible to its earlier state.

Quite aside from its history as a respectable residence of a prominent citizen, the house played a shady role during the bootlegging period. It was then occupied by the owner of a mortuary, who kept a hearse and spare caskets in the basement. These were a front for a lucrative liquor business. The hearse is supposed to have transported whiskey, landed at North Beach. Bottling was done in the house, it was alleged. A nuisance suit filed by neighbors terminated this chapter of the mansion's chronicle.

J. C. Saunders was a one-time collector of customs at Port Townsend and president of the Commercial Bank. He erected the house (upper on page 92) in 1889 and sent to Spain for the stained glass windows. The house has seven fireplaces, one in the dining room with a 22-inch-deep niche (shown above) in the chimney to accommodate an art glass panel. Plain glass had been inserted at the time this photograph was made, but the present owners found the panel and have restored it.

Saunders was a Southern gentleman and the story goes that he and his wife did not agree as to the style of their new home; one wanted it Georgian, the other Victorian. So it is Victorian on the outside, Georgian on the inside. Its former severe decor is hard to distinguish now, as it is being operated as

Holly Manor, a sightseeing attraction on a conducted-tour basis. The owners have filled it with antique furnishings.

Architecturally one of its features is the use of remarkable curved shingling in front on the third floor porch.

Saunders lost his home during the hard times of 1893 and went away. A distant relation remembered that the house was so cold in winter the family generally moved into town during the chilly season.

This mansion is in the country on the south side of Port Townsend, in the same sightly area as Manresa Hall, the former Eisenbeis residence.

Port Townsend, Queen Anne cottage at 1519 Washington Street, constructed in 1879 by John Frye. This house, which stood on the old F. W. Pettygrove tract, was occupied from 1930 to 1968 by the Maloney sisters.

Eisenbeis Castle is the older portion of Manresa Hall, until recently a Jesuit formation school on the slope of the hill south of Port Townsend.

Charles Eisenbeis, a master baker from Prussia, was the town's first mayor. He arrived there in 1858 and opened a shop to manufacture crackers and ship bread. Two years later he moved to Steilacoom, had a bakery there, then returned to Port Townsend five years later and stayed the remainder of his life. He died in 1902.

Eisenbeis platted real estate tracts and erected business blocks, including the first stone building on Water Street in 1873. He also built the Mount Baker block. He was interested in a brewery, brick yard, lumber mill, wharves and banks and he built a great hotel on the hill which never was occupied, owing to the financial crash.

At the peak of the boom in 1892 Eisenbeis erected his three-story brick and stone residence roofed with slate. It has three turrets across the front and suggests a Rhine castle.

The old section of Manresa Hall consisted of a basement, three floors and attic, all of sturdy construction, with finely crafted hardware, redwood and oak paneling and tile fireplaces. It was purchased in 1925 by the Jesuits and a south wing was added and the entire combined structure was given a uniform coat of stucco. The building was sold late in 1968 to Mr. and Mrs. Joshua North owners of a Port Townsend restaurant who planned to remodel the place into an inn. The chapel which had been desanctified will become a dining room, with the former choir loft converted into a cocktail lounge.

"Frank's Folly" is the nickname given the house at 313 Walker Street, Port Townsend, now owned by Mr. and Mrs. James Daubenberger. Sometimes it is referred to as the old German consulate.

The exterior was completed in 1890 but the interior was not finished until the present century. Frank A. Hastings, who started the turreted mansion, never was able to see it through. After seven years of nonpayment of taxes, C. A. Olson purchased the shell of the house in 1904 at a county sale for $2,500. It included six lots and a large completed carriage house or barn. At the sale Olson won out against a man who was bidding with the idea of tearing down the residence for its lumber.

Olson wished to finish the house as originally planned and went to Hastings to buy the blueprints, but the latter refused, so the new owner set to work to complete it as best he could with the help of Julius Sather. Except for the kitchen, dining room and one living room, nothing had been started. There were no windows, stairs or walls, just uprights and some shiplap flooring. The Hastings had lived in the two and a half partially-finished rooms and had obtained water from a cistern just outside the back door.

It was two years more before the work was completed. Olson, at that time county assessor, in his spare hours did some of the carpentering and Sather did the rest. Outsiders were hired to pour cement and do the plastering.

The woodwork was oak, which Sather hand-rubbed. The plastered walls were then papered. In the drawing room is a chandelier in grape vine design, purchased in Seattle. It had been ordered for the Rathskeller restaurant and refused because it was not large enough. Olson saw it and purchased it in 1905 for $125. The showy fixture was reported erroneously to have come from the Alaska Yukon Pacific Exposition.

Several small fireplaces were in the house, but now only two principal ones remain.

Granite for the foundation and outside pillars was cut from a granite pit across the street.

The barn, originally located on the northwest corner of the lots, apparently never was used for horses. Olson sold it to N. W. O'Rear, a customs service officer, who moved it to the two lots behind the house which he purchased. He added windows and porches and made the building into a seven-room residence.

The Olson-Hastings house became known as the German consulate through August Duddenhausen, a pensioned Civil War veteran who had lost a leg in the war. He worked in the court house and invested his small income at county sales of acreage. When he could no longer work he moved to the Olson home and his pension went mostly to pay taxes on his land, all of which he finally lost. Meanwhile the Olsons fed and clothed him and in the end buried him.

When the customs house was moved to Seattle the German consul requested Duddenhausen to take care of minor matters in Port Townsend. He served as vice consul a year and a half, transacting what little official business he had in the Olsons' parlor.

One other German name is associated with the house. When Count Felix von Luckner, the famous First World War raider, was a youth of 16 he shipped on a sailing vessel. It arrived in Port Townsend at a time when von Luckner heard that he had inherited an estate in Germany. The young man jumped ship and appealed to Duddenhausen to loan him $10 to get him to the consulate in Seattle. Duddenhausen refused, but Mrs. Olson felt sorry for the lad, hid him two days in the basement until his ship departed, then loaned him the fare to Seattle.

The third floor of the house is remarkable for being completely finished. The front turret has a splendid view of the harbor. The room this tower adjoins has arc-shaped windows which frame the panorama on either side of the chimney.

The once-upon-a-time carriage house no longer is painted the same color as the mansion, but otherwise its exterior is not greatly changed. Its mansard dome originally had four small dormer windows instead of two and there was another little quadrangular turret near the chimney.

Chevy Chase, a resort on Port Discovery Bay, represents three stages of home-building on the Quimper Peninsula, for it is comprised of a trio of houses ranging from a very old homestead cabin to a stately mansion of the 1890's, complete with widow's walk.

The three structures are all on the former homestead of John F. Tukey, who arrived from Maine as one of the crew of a vessel that took on a cargo of ship knees and timbers on the bay in 1850. He left the ship and marked out a land claim on the rainy slope of Cry Baby Mountain (Mount Chatham). He sold the tract two years later and staked a donation claim on the bay shore, where he continued to live the remainder of his life. In 1880 he married a Port Townsend widow, Mrs. Chase, whose daughter, Miss Mary Chase, made the place over into a hostelry that was celebrated locally. She ran the resort from 1913 to 1946, when the property was sold to Philip Bailey of Seattle.

The inn made use of all of the buildings on the property, the pioneer cabin serving first as living quarters, later as the wash house. The second home

supplied sleeping space for guests. It bears a plaque over the door, stating that Tukey used it as his homestead house. The large mansion became the inn proper, with dining and social halls.

Ever since 1862 it has been believed that a stolen treasure was buried on this property. Tukey one day saw two Indians and a white man bring a heavy chest ashore by canoe and carry it into a timbered portion of his farm. The white man later was arrested and identified as an absconding Canadian paymaster from Victoria who made off with 6,000 gold sovereigns that never were found. He was sentenced to a long prison term. No one knew if he returned afterward and dug up his horde. Others, including Tukey, hunted it for years.

Port Gamble

Port Gamble's landscape has not changed much with the passage of the years. Though none of the first houses on the sandspit below the town survived, some buildings dating from the 1870's and 1880's are well preserved. Rainier Avenue, with its row of cottages with steeply pitched roofs, its elm trees and New England-style church, is reminiscent of East Machias, Maine, from which the town's founders came.

Port Gamble was and still is exclusively company owned, the business and social buildings and all but two of its houses (and these are on 99-year-lease land) being on property of Pope and Talbot, proprietors of the sawmill in Gamble Bay. In 1853 Captain William C. Talbot went in a schooner to Puget Sound and chose this harbor as a suitable site for a sawmill. The first buildings erected here were of split cedar boards and Eastern lumber. When the

schooner departed a crew stayed on to cut foundation timbers for the mill, machinery for which already was on the way.

The first little mill was replaced six years later with a new one. Altogether six mills have stood at the same location. While the mills have changed, the main street has remained the same. Other buildings in the town have been removed, but the row of white houses now seems assured of indefinite survival, since it has been designated a national historic site.

A modified New England salt box, the M. S. Drew house, below, sits by the main thoroughfare of Port Gamble. It was erected in 1870 for the Pope and Talbot Company's log agent and is the longest occupied of any of the houses in town. It has one of the plainest interiors.

The kitchen wing was built on, some other room perhaps serving this purpose at first.

A few years ago the company intended to remove most of the old houses as they became vacant, but since Port Gamble has been designated a national historic site an effort is being made to keep them in good shape and fully occupied.

In line with this, reconstruction is under way on the James Thompson home, more than a century old, which reverted to the company after expiration of the 99-year lease. The rear portion had to be removed and rebuilt because of deterioration of the wood. An old photograph has been guiding the carpenters in the work of restoration.

Mr. and Mrs. Frank Anton lived in the D. L. Jackson house. The latter was postmaster for many years. He had a son who went to Seattle, then returned to port Gamble also as postmaster. He wanted to live in the old family home and had to pay rent to do so, as it was on company land.

The Nystrom house at right also is on Rainer Avenue. The oldest building there is the church.

Another house stands beside the service station and is occupied by the Epperson family. A sign on the outside bears the date 1873 and says that William Gove, captain of the tugs *Goliah, Tyee* and *Wanderer* lived there.

At least 30 of the old houses gradually were demolished by the company as they presented maintenance problems. It cost more to keep them up than they were worth. The sentiment has changed recently and an effort is being made to save as many as possible. In the center of town are eight old houses, with five others a few blocks away.

The square one in the immediate foreground of this picture was brought by barge from Port Ludlow in 1935. It was erected in the early 1900's.

Mrs. Thomas Driscoll, wife of Pope and Talbot's chief forester at Port Gamble, is quite accustomed to showing her home to tour parties. She has endeavored to trace the history of the place, built about 1887, but has been unable to discover whether it was occupied first by E. G. Ames, general manager, or William Walker, brother of Cyrus Walker, who long ago had a house that stood almost in front of this one. Cyrus moved to Port Ludlow to a great mansion, now gone.

Ceilings are 10 feet high and the residence is hard to heat, but well worth some inconvenience, Mrs. Driscoll said, because it is so spacious. The solid walls make for a quiet house. One can pound nails anywhere.

The Driscolls do not risk using the fireplaces because of earthquake damage to chimneys, but they keep the hearths as they were. The living room fireplace is of carved mahogany with shelves above and at the sides, wood pillars and fancy tiles of the same color. The family room fireplace is of carved oak with green tiles.

Another fireplace is in wood, perhaps walnut, with pillars shaped like plump buttressed piano legs. The tiles in two colors represent a continuous design of two pots of flowers, one on either side of the fire. The hearth has eight colors of tiles.

The oak fireplace in the front bed room has rose tiles, two brackets over two triangular shaped mirrors, a shelf over the main central mirror and floral carvings continuous in the panels around the fire-opening. This is a charming room with a balcony over a bay window and a splendid view.

The front entrance is elaborate, with an eight-foot door and a vestibule. The outer door has red, white and blue etched glass and the inner door has six colors of glass in its square lights.

On the stairway are five panels in many-colored glass. The railing is mahogany and the newel post on the landing is topped with a bronze urn with four flower-shaped light fixtures.

All of the doors have medallions on the upper corners of the moldings. There are about 150 medallions in the house, even in closets, and Mrs. Driscoll found spares tucked away in the basement. The 35 doors are paneled and have metal knobs with a pebbled finish and beveled rim.

Clothes closets are cedar lined and have windows. The bath room has stained glass windows and fancy metal drawer pulls on the built-ins. The attic is neatly carpentered and apparently was used for dancing. Its storage space consists of closed cupboards. A maid's room is at one side. The third floor is well lighted, with windows of several shapes, one an arc, others triangles.

Hood Canal

Seabeck, in Western Kitsap County, was a logging community built around a mill that commenced operating in July, 1857. Its ruling spirit, Marshall Blinn, principal owner, named the place for his former home town in Maine. In 1865 he added a shipyard and in 1883 a second sawmill opened. By the latter date Blinn had sold his interest in the Washington Mill Co. and moved away. He had attempted to run a temperance town, but after his departure it became wide open and had four saloons.

On August 6, 1886 the mill, dock, shipyard and ships burned in a tremendous fire and Seabeck, the liveliest community of Hood Canal and on much of Puget Sound, became a ghost town. It was visited by a few campers and boatmen.

The first returning sign of life was when A. L. Hotchkin at the beginning of the century bought the old company store and reopened it. For a time a cross-canal ferry was operated and stages ran to Seabeck. In 1914 Lawrence J. and George Colman of Seattle purchased most of the townsite to establish an interdenominational campground for church conferences and religious organizations.

In and around Seabeck one can see the millwork, windows and doors that were brought from the East for some of the initial structures.

Many of the loggers who came to the Pacific Coast were from Maine, among them a number of carpenters who were fairly good designers. In such early mill towns in Washington the carpenters worked winters on the houses when the weather was too inclement for being in the woods.

If Seabeck houses followed a simple pattern, as this one does, they made up for the lack of ornament with a million-dollar view of the Olympic Range.

The cook house (now Seabeck's meeting house) in early days was presided over by a Chinese, Ah Fong, noted for his thrift.

There was no bank in the logging town and when payrolls were late in coming by ship from San Francisco, says Gordon Newell in his historical pamphlet on Seabeck, the mill management was in the habit of securing a temporary loan from Ah Fong. He could produce as much as $5,000 by simply disappearing in the forest and bringing back the required amount in $20 gold pieces.

One day he went to his private bank in the woods and never returned. He is said to have been murdered for his money, much of which still may be buried on the hill behind the town.

Marshall Blinn's mill pond became a swimming pool. The cookhouse became the meeting house. The United States Hotel became the inn on the grounds. The counter where guests register was the bar, installed in defiance of Blinn's temperance principles.

A second fire in 1957 destroyed more of the old town, but the conference buildings survived.

The rustic charm of this farm house at Eldon is largely due to its location beside Hood Canal. The place was started in 1895 on a much smaller scale by Albert Schaufler, who had come to the United States after serving in the German army. A tinsmith, he had taken a 160-acre timber claim near Hama Hama.

When he married he suddenly acquired a large family, for his wife was the former Mrs. Homberg, a Swedish widow with seven children. The Schauflers had five more after that.

In 1905 Schaufler decided to enlarge his house and make it into a picturesque lodge where he could rent rooms to hunting parties and surveyors who were often through the Olympic Peninsula. He towed the necessary lumber up Hood Canal in a raft.

Schaufler enjoyed only a few years in his new role of host to hunters. He died in 1909. His family continued to live in the house another 20 years, then after Mrs. Schaufler's death it was purchased by C. R. Diesen, the present occupant.

paddled by canoe back and forth in order to improve his farm and build a cabin.

He added steadily to his acres, buying school and railroad land-grant property and that of other settlers until by 1884 he had a total of more than 900 acres.

In 1876 he married a widow, Mrs. Amanda Knox Leake, whose father was agent on the nearby Indian reservation. She displayed great facility with the native jargon and quickly became interpreter. She had two little sons by her first marriage and five more children by Webb. The small house by the river was so crowded he built another in the more pretentious Gothic style on higher ground to escape floods. It is now a ruin standing at the junction of Union Road and one leading across the river.

The family went to Seattle for a time, moved back after the 1889 fire and Webb built his third home near the site of his son Tom's brick house. The ranch prospered, raising hay, potatoes and vegetables for logging camps and furnishing pasture for cattle and horses.

The greater portion of the south side of the Lower Skokomish River was owned and developed by the Thomas Webb family. The house below is the second residence Tom built for them.

Webb, born in Ireland in 1827, emigrated to Ontario, Canada and in 1853 journeyed west, driving a team of oxen for a man who had a long train of wagons headed for California. Webb left there and walked from Portland to Puget Sound and took a donation claim on the Skokomish. His patent was dated 1855. He worked in a Port Ludlow mill and

This farm house, owned by Marvin Lorenzen at Brinnon in Southeastern Jefferson County, was built by the community's namesake, Elwell P. Brinnon. He homesteaded the property in 1875 and owned most of the land on the flat at the mouth of the Dosewallips River.

Brinnon died in 1895, leaving his home to his widow, Kate, who sold it three years later to Chester Gilbert. It changed hands again and again, but for 20 years was owned by Thomas Miller.

Some time between 1935 and 1940 the house was jacked up and a full basement was put in while John Miller was the owner. The house was remodelled about three times. The original building was absorbed into the present one but its outlines are visible in the left hand gable. The dwelling is the oldest in Brinnon.

Here is a mention of it from a young girl's diary of the early 1890's: "The footpath turns and goes past the Brinnon place. I always walk carefully and fast past here because Mrs. Brinnon is an Indian. There are lace curtains at the windows and they say Mr. Brinnon is rich. But we will keep going because his wife is an Indian. I've never seen an Indian, but I am afraid of her."

John McReavy, born in Northfield, Me. in 1840, left there when he was 21. He bought a logging camp at Allyn on credit and when he was out of debt moved his outfit to Union River and logged continuously until he sold in 1886 to the Puget Mill Co. He made several fortunes and lost them. He was active in affairs of the newly-launched State of Washington, a member of the constitutional convention, a senator and member of the State Capitol Commission.

To supply his loggers with farm produce McReavy diked and cleared 400 acres and by the '90s he had a famous ranch. He also bought the Trading Post at Union City.

His original logging railroad ran on wooden rails stripped with metal and the cars were pulled by oxen.

In 1870 McReavy married his wife, Fanny, and settled her in a block house of hewn timbers a foot thick and twice as wide. They lived in it five years then went into a home built by Fanny's father, Warren Gove, in 1875. Next year the old block house was torn down. No one knew who had built it. Many bullets were imbedded in the timbers.

The Union Pacific was looking for a terminus and Union City was one of the places under consideration. While the boom lasted McReavy built the mansion on the hill. It had an orchard and landscaped garden. In front of the house was the "courting tree," a maple which grew to 60 feet in spread and eventually contained a round platform and stairs leading to a space where eight or nine persons could sit.

The McReavys moved into the house about 1890 at the height of prosperity. Although the panic of 1893 turned Union City into a ghost town, John McReavy stayed on and spent his declining years in the house, enjoying his garden. He died in 1918. His daughter lives today in the old home.

Pacific County

Although R. H. Espy was a founder of Oysterville, arriving there in 1854, he made do with a log cabin until 1871, when he built this home facing the waterfront. It once looked out upon a street, long since washed away by the winter storms on Willapa Bay.

Espy built the house for his bride, Julia, who had been a school teacher. The kitchen and bed room wing were remodeled and an earlier porch was converted into a dining room. Originally there were three upstairs bed rooms, but the alterations provided for six.

It is recalled that when a square piano was purchased in San Francisco, in order to get it into the parlor the long windows had to be removed and the instrument, turned on its side, was carried through.

A feature of the sitting room is a fireplace faced with slate. It is flush with the wall, except for a small mantel, and is recessed between book shelves and, on the rear side of the wall in the adjoining room, a chimney cupboard. The walnut stair rail is beautifully finished. Several of the old oil hanging lamps are still in the house.

Espy was a pioneer oyster man, who was told of the location of choice oyster beds by an Indian chief.

The house always has belonged in the same family and today is occupied by his youngest son, Cecil Espy.

Oysterville had an entire street of picturesque houses, which until a few years ago were not much changed from their original condition. However, time and damp weather have taken their toll and those still inhabited for the most part have undergone alterations and extensive repairs.

Outstanding are the two houses built by the Crellin brothers, John and Thomas, prosperous oystermen. The family came from the Isle of Man and was the only one to arrive in Oysterville with ample funds.

The first brother to build a home of his own was John, who in 1873 erected this roomy mansion, which formerly had a front porch facing Willapa Bay. The main entrance is now the rear one, toward the street.

The Crellins moved away long ago to San Francisco, where they continued in the oyster business. Since 1920 John's dwelling has belonged to the Heckes family, who for many years operated a summer boarding house in it. So popular was the place that additional kitchen and dining accommodations were added in a wing to the right. The establishment overflowed into the village and the Heckes' boarders often were lodged in other homes in the immediate vicinity.

John Crellin built well, employing redwood lumber from Eureka, Calif. In his yard he planted seedling Garry pines from San Francisco. These great trees are distinguishing features of the place. Other features are the ornamental bargeboards, the arched window upstairs in front, a finely turned

stair railing, panelled doors and chimney cup-boards.

During the years when the Heckes operated their country inn they assembled many antique furnishings in keeping with the setting. Some interesting pieces remain in possession of Mr. and Mrs. Glen Heckes, the present occupants. The old dining room still is a show place. Mrs. Heckes, in addition, owns a large collection of antique bottles, many dug from the beach where Oysterville's pioneer bars once stood.

Today the family lives entirely downstairs for the sake of greater comfort. The walls upstairs are as they were originally- flowered wallpaper over muslin and beneath these only the redwood boards. Mrs. Heckes tells a story about the bed room with the Gothic window.

"Years ago," she related, "an evangelist was holding meetings on the beach and people of Oysterville took turns giving him a room. We hadn't been forward about offering, but intended to take our turn. We got this room ready for him and the night be-fore he was due to come something unexpected happened.

"For a long time we had been hearing what we thought was a squirrel in the attic just off this room. We thought it would be a good thing to get it out before the evangelist came, so we put a black kitten through the panel opening that led to the space under the rafters. Some time after we'd gone to bed the cat pounced and a sickening wave of odor came out. Those thin cloth walls held back nothing. We realized right away that our squirrel was an entirely different breed. The kitten was scared and we had a terrible time coaxing it out. Then my aunts tried everything anyone could suggest to get rid of the smell. They burned rags and coffee in the room, but none of their measures did any good.

"We excused ourselves to the minister and told him there'd been a skunk in the wall and he couldn't possibly sleep here, but I'm sure he never believed us. He must have thought we made up the story to avoid taking him in."

A long, lacey fretwork trim adorns the gables of the house which for many years was occupied by the late Harry Espy, of Oysterville. It was built in 1874 by Thomas Crellin, who outdid his brother, John, and had the structure plastered throughout.

Like his father, Harry Espy engaged in the oyster business. He was one of seven children, the one who stayed in home territory; the others moved away to marry or follow other lines of business. Harry also had been away as a mining engineer, but upon his father's taking ill, set out for Oysterville to stay a few weeks—and never left. One of his wife's first remembered sights there was during a winter storm seeing a girl rowing a boat up the main street.

The family witnessed the decline of the oyster industry and its rejuvenation through the planting of Japanese seed. Though the town was almost dead, its houses abandoned, the oyster beds came alive again and Espy was well justified in having had faith in them so many years.

History of the oldest house in Oysterville is lost and its exact age is undetermined though it dates from about 1865. It was for a long time property of the Morgan Oyster Co. and many tenants have lived in it. Particularly it seems to have attracted newlyweds. The present owner is Mona Espy Seymour.

"**Whatever Dad built** had to be perfect and it had to be solid. We used to say if he put up anything you couldn't tear it down; you'd have to burn it," said the daughter of S. L. Mathews, whose home this was. The cottage stands on Ocean Park's main crossroad and its many windows have attracted the curiosity of the Long Beach Peninsula's summer vacationers.

Mathews, who was a native of Booth Bay Harbor, Maine, built the house like one he had admired there. The lumber was brought by scow from South Bend and hauled overland from Nahcotta. The port hole may have been an afterthought, the product of a beachcombing foray following a shipwreck. But the round-topped glass panes were cut by Mathews in his own workshop and were meticulously framed by him. His wife approved the arrangement, for she was a flower lover and the year around plants, sheltered from chill winds, thrived in pots behind the windows.

Mathews moved from Oysterville to Ocean Park in 1888 and began his house three years later. He worked at it the next two years in between times

building many other cottages on the beach—he is said to have built half of Ocean Park.

Trees stood close around the home when the Mathews family moved in and the father used to be afraid of some of them falling on it at night during storms.

Mathews was noted for his Yankee wit, but he took his house seriously and it was one subject about which he cracked no jokes.

Mr. and Mrs. Fred Colbert moved to Ilwaco in 1883 from old Chinook, where they had lived since their marriage 13 years earlier. Their source of income had been from seining salmon along the shore in front of the village, but when fish traps were introduced in Baker's Bay and a cannery built at Ilwaco many fishermen, Colbert included, decided to try their luck with the new method. He bought lots from Isaac Whealdon, who had platted part of his land claim into a townsite. Since lumber was scarce, Colbert decided to take down his former home and bring the salvaged lumber to the new location.

His Ilwaco house began with what is now the middle section. It was a plain box type of structure, a story and a half high, with walls of fir planks placed upright and fastened with square nails. Across the salvaged boards a covering of overlapping siding was nailed into place. In areas where winter storms struck hardest an extra covering of cedar shingles was added to keep out the cold. A lean-to was built across the north side to serve as kitchen. Then the family of four daughters and a son moved in.

Before long the house was a tight fit after two more daughters were born, so it was decided to build on another addition. The lean-to kitchen was torn down and a long ell replaced it, containing a large dining room, kitchen, pantry and bath. Upstairs was one long room where Mrs. Colbert kept her quilting frame and sewing machine. Each winter much time was spent up there knitting web for the next season's fish traps. Many hundreds of pounds of cotton twine were carried up the back stairs to the work room, where the father, mother and four grown daughters did the knitting. Younger members of the family sometimes balled the twine and filled the needles for the knitters.

Fancy shingles were popular in the '90s and Fred Colbert had the east side of the house covered with them. With the main building extended on both sides four stoves were needed for heat—the cook stove in the kitchen and heaters in the parlor, sitting room and upstairs work room. These required the three chimneys still standing.

To this day the house belongs to surviving members of the Colbert family and, although they only spend summers and autumns there, they consider it home. The barn for two horses and a cow and the chicken house are gone, but many of the tall poplar trees planted by Mrs. Colbert are standing. During the severe storm of 1962 some fruit and shade trees were destroyed. The house never has been rented and remains almost unchanged, a delightful souvenir of Ilwaco's past.

Still serving a useful purpose in the community of Bay Center is the home James P. Goodpasture built on his arrival there in 1873. The settlement was then called Palux, but the name was changed two years later. Oysters had attracted the original inhabitants and the bivalves were long the basis of the town's commercial life. By the mid 1880's it had 400 inhabitants, five stores, a restaurant, hotel and four churches.

Goodpasture, born in Iowa in 1848, moved to Oregon when a young man. He soon found his way to Bay Center and lived there continuously from 1873 to 1901. His house was the second oldest, the only other dwelling being that of A. S. Bush. Today the Bush house is gone. This one was standing empty when a few years ago a building was needed for a branch of the county library. Hope Wilson Clark, librarian, offered the use of the old house and has made its main room into an attractive meeting place for Bay Centerites.

The house was built by Goodpasture's own hands, as he was a knowledgeable carpenter in addition to being a farmer and storekeeper.

Officers' houses at Fort Columbia State Park, east of Chinook. The one nearest is the State Parks Museum; the other to the right (the commanding officer's residence) is furnished in the period of the fort and maintained by the Daughters of the American Revolution. The buildings were completed in 1902. They are of the same vintage as the barracks and hospital.

The first real garrison arrived at Fort Columbia in June, 1903. Until the First World War generally four officers and 100 men were stationed there. Outbreak of hostilities brought a considerable expansion of the harbor defenses, the fort was renovated and modernized, but at the end of the conflict it was almost completely deactivated. Once again during the Second World War the place was rehabilitated. But such defenses are outdated and in 1947 the post was declared surplus property and a major portion was transferred to the State of Washington. It is now a historical state park and a designated national historic site.

The right-hand portion of Tokeland's venerable hotel was the pioneer home of the Kindred family. Toke Point had been homesteaded in 1858 by George Brown, whose daughter, Elizabeth, in 1880 married William S. Kindred. His parents had migrated to Oregon in 1844 with the Michael Simmons party.

The young couple made their home at Tokeland and Kindred purchased his father-in-law's holdings, his dairying and oyster business. A new house was next on the agenda and in 1885 lumber was obtained from a South Bend mill and the present west wing was erected.

After having often put up travelers, the Kindreds decided to open an inn in 1899. They enlarged the farm house and again added to it in 1910. The hotel first attracted residents of South Bend, Raymond and Grays Harbor communities, but after a time patrons came from as far away as Idaho, Eastern Washington and Southern California. In its heyday Kindred drove a horse-drawn tallyho to the dock to meet guests and pick up freight from boats that ran to South Bend and Nahcotta.

The inn was famous for its food. Poultry and beef were raised on the big farm, there were always oysters and Indians kept the kitchen well supplied with fresh razor clams, crabs and fish.

Since 1943, after Kindred's death, ownership passed outside the family.

John Russell in 1891 built this home in South Bend's Alta Vista (High View), where the land was to be kept choice and houses would not be in rows. This one is a landmark that can be seen from far away. It overlooks many miles of the Willapa River Valley.

In 1903 the house was purchased by S. H. Eichner, banker, who came from the East during the boom of 1891. It was for many years the Eichners' home and after his death his widow rented it.

The Edward D. Buell home at Menlo, Pacific County, was built in 1885 a few feet from where Willapa Valley's first and only blockhouse stood. Though modernized by the present occupants, the dwelling retains the atmosphere of earlier times.

The farm has been in the ownership of the same family more than a century. Mrs. Buell is the great grandniece of Christian Giesy, who settled there in 1854 with the advance guard of the historic Keil colony.

The colonizing project, directed by Dr. William Keil, arrived from Bethel, Mo. the following year, but the leader was displeased with what he saw and did not stay. He transferred his colony shortly to Aurora, Ore., but left behind a melancholy reminder of his visit.

Up a steep path across a pasture to the east of the house is a graveyard with 25 headstones, all but two of which are those of Giesys. The oldest inscribed stone marks the burial place of young Willie Kiel, who died just before the main vanguard set forth from Missouri. His body traveled 1,800 miles across the United States in a lead coffin filled with alcohol, riding in an ambulance wagon at the head of the train of prairie schooners.

Christian Giesy who had gone in advance with eight others to seek a suitable place for settlement in the Far West, met the cavalcade at The Dalles and accompanied it to the Willapa. Willie was buried there November 25, 1855.

Seven claims were taken in the valley by members of the Giesy family. Sebastian Giesy lived the longest, moving on the property Dr. Kiel turned over to his brother, John Giesy, and building the present house.

Dr. Kiel had no objection of the Giesys staying where they were and permitted them to pay back community funds they had laid out for the claims. The first school and the first post office in the valley were in this house.

Sebastian Giesy arrived in the 1855 train and built a mill later between the Buell home and Menlo. The house stands where the party landed and Christian had built the blockhouse. While construction of the new home was in progress the blockhouse was moved forward on the property and the family lived in it temporarily. Mrs. Buell remembered when a little girl she had seen post holes of the old stockade and heard her mother tell about it.

The Giesy house was noted always for hospitality and was a stopover place where travelers could be sure of a warm bed, a good meal or a cup of coffee.

Wahkiakum, Clark, Cowlitz and Lewis Counties

Well past the centenarian mark is the home of Congresswoman Julia Butler Hansen at Cathlamet. It was built about 1860 on part of the James Birnie donation claim for John Fitzpatrick, a pioneer salmon seiner and salter on the Columbia River.

It was among Cathlamet's first three houses and is the only one remaining of the trio. Birnie, born in Scotland, arrived on the Columbia in 1818 with the North West Company and was their trader at The Dalles and later clerk at Fort George (Astoria). He continued to be employed in the fur trade after the Hudson's Bay Company took over the posts, retiring from the service in 1846. He moved that year by canoe to Cathlamet, built a house called Birnie's Retreat and lived there with his 13 children. He packed salted salmon and conducted a trading store.

Judge William Strong was the second settler at Cathlamet, building on the point. Between these two homes stood the Fitzgerald house, which in 1871 became the property of Mrs. George S. Roberts. Roberts had married Birnie's only sister, Rose, when she journeyed out from Scotland to become the first teacher for the Birnie children.

Roberts took his bride to his post at Cowlitz Farm, a Hudson's Bay subsidiary, where he was in charge. His first wife died while he was stationed there.

After settlement of the British claims Roberts moved to Cathlamet and operated a store. He died in 1883 and two years later James F. Kimball, grandfather of Mrs. Hansen, purchased the home. He was a logger from Maine who reached Olympia in 1877 and made several moves before settling at Cathlamet. When his family moved in, the upstairs of the house was a large loft that had been used for dances.

"My grandmother," related Mrs. Hansen, "had it divided into bed rooms by a carpenter son-in-law of James Birnie. Her New England disgust at his car-

penter ability was immense and as a little girl I heard her growling many times about his way of hanging doors.

"The oldest part of the house is built of cedar straight board construction and when we have been doing repair work, we have discovered that these boards are just as white as the day they were put in. The walls are filled with square nails. The timbers between floors are of an unusual thickness and undoubtedly were milled either at Westport or at James Birnie's old sawmill, which was across the river.

"The front door once faced the Columbia, as the main trail was between the Strong house on the point below and Birnie's on the hill, with our house between and the Indian village a little to the southeast of us."

Two pear trees in the yard came from the early orchard at Fort Vancouver. Roberts, a true horticulturist, set out trees and plants extensively. The last of his cherry trees was a victim of the big blowdown of Columbus Day, 1962. The large birch in the front yard was planted by Mrs. Hansen's grandmother, who was from New Hampshire.

"I'm tired of looking at evergreens and I want something that reminds me of New England," she declared.

In the back of the house are the original square-paned windows. To wash them, one can take out a strip of wood and remove the window.

Inside, the house has been modernized, but is laid out much the same as when Mrs. Hansen was a little girl. The original woodwork has been retained upstairs. Mrs. Hansen's father, a contractor, put in many of the improvements before the turn of the century.

Much Cathlamet history is associated with the house. Roberts was active in county affairs and persons came and went who were part of early life on the river.

About 1890, when it was decided to plat the town, Colonel Whitfield, a veteran of General Robert E. Lee's Northern Virginia staff, arrived to do this, bringing his wife, Medora. As there were no hotels in Cathlamet the colonel and his lady were invited to stay with the Kimballs.

"The interesting part of this particular arrangement," Mrs. Hansen explained, "was that my grandfather was a veteran of Sherman's army that marched through Georgia. He and Colonel Whitfield of the Confederate army became fast friends. In fact, the colonel used our house as the center for his platting when he laid out the town."

The Slocum House in Esther Short Park, Vancouver, built about 1867 by Charles W. and Laura Slocum, follows a Rhode Island pattern of architecture reminiscent of the owner's home in the East. From the widow's walk it was possible to see far up and down the Columbia River when the home was on its former site, a block distant. The house was moved to the park in 1966 with funds raised by popular subscription and is maintained by the Old Slocum House Theatre Company under a five-year contract.

Described as a modified Italianate villa, it has a curving stairway, circular entrance hall, doors 12 feet high, ceiling medallions and a pair of octagonal rooms with marble fireplaces. The pioneer merchant owner had a love of fine wood and cabinet work.

Theatrical presentations are given in the small auditorium. Productions for children are planned and there will be other uses for meeting rooms and the basement workshop.

Quarters for the commanding general at Vancouver Barracks, upper right, were erected in 1886. The structure, at present occupied by the Red Cross, is called the Marshall House because General George C. Marshall lived there on a tour of duty. All of the buildings on the military reservation except this and the Grant house are owned by the Veterans Administration and occupied by members of the hospital staff.

None of the structures had central heating until after 1900 and all rooms were warmed with fireplaces and stoves. A requisite of officers' quarters was always some tucked-away chambers for servants, for whom allowances were made in earlier days.

Officers enjoyed an active social life and calling cards were as important to them as a dress sword. Vancouver was for many years classed as a most desirable station.

Here is a visitor's description of the commandant's house as it was in 1896:

"This was a large mansion, situated west of the parade ground. Its tastefully furnished apartments, opening pleasantly into one another, had an air of permanency, quite different from the simple style of living civilians associate with Army quarters and which as a rule is imposed by the exigencies of Army life. In due course of time (the guests) were introduced to an immensely broad verandah, covered with vines on one side, effectively shielding them from the gaze of passersby, and here, seated in fours at little tables, they partook of a dainty luncheon and at the same time listened to a succession of lively pieces played by the 14th Infantry band ... Their eyes also had a treat, for from their seats they could see Mt. Hood, across whose snowy surface a band of white clouds lingered, as if partially obscuring it, to enhance its loveliness."

Dr. R. D. Wiswall House

Very impressive for its tower is the home at the northeast corner of Thirteenth and Esther Streets, Vancouver, generally associated with Dr. R. D. Wiswall's family, who have owned it since 1918.

The mansion was designed in 1891 by O. M. Hidden, architect, for W. Byron Daniels, who served terms as mayor of Vancouver and as a member of the state legislature.

Much scrollwork went into the gables of this residence and the ridgepoles, in their original state, were adorned with elaborate cresting. The entire second floor was finished with fancy-butt shingles. The cupalo has spindles and arches and is topped with a carved filagree post. Behind the home is a carriage house.

Inside the dwelling are 13 rooms. The third floor is unfinished except for one small bed room. Ceiling and dado of the entrance hall are of beautiful oak paneling. The stair railing is also of oak. Much of the hand-carved woodwork was prepared on the premises.

The living room and master's bedroom have fireplaces of Italian tiles. The trim and screens for

The W. F. Hidden House

warm-weather use are of cast ornamental bronze.

Dr. Wiswall was the second member of the Washington Legislature to occupy the house. He was a prominent physician of Vancouver, a graduate of the University of Oregon Medical School in 1897.

Signs on this structure at 13th and Main Streets, Vancouver were changed shortly after the photographer was there and it is now the Altes Haus, a German restaurant.

It was built in 1883 by Lowell Mason Hidden, who bought the land more than a century ago. For 77 years the residence had a hand-split, hand-shaved cedar roof, replaced in 1961. The woodwork inside is ash, with walnut trim. The original stained glass and shutters are still to be seen. Architect for the place was Oliver Moody Hidden. Residence, barn and rock wall are said to have cost $10,000, an impressive sum at that time.

L. M. Hidden lived first in a log cabin at 14th and Main. He was extremely thrifty as a young man and after buying his property in 1865 he cut wood for steamers and made pickets for government fences. He helped dig a ditch for Vancouver's first water system and prepared decking for the first city dock. Meanwhile he farmed and, as a sideline in 1870-71, ran the old Pacific House because the town needed a hotel. It was while he and his wife were in it that their son, William Foster Hidden was born.

Immediately afterward Lowell Hidden began producing brick at 15th and Main, near the present Clark County Museum. Two large buildings were then under construction and brick for them had to be brought from Portland. Hidden saw to it that after that his name was left in the brick walls of many Vancouver structures. His firm turned out 300,000 hand-made bricks for Providence Academy and 900,000 for the Tacoma Hotel, also brick for the first paper mill at Camas.

Hidden at the time of his death in 1923 was president of the United States National Bank of Vancouver. He was known as a public benefactor; he found land for the School for the Deaf, gave a site for the public library, was one of the founders of the Clark County Fair and a promoter of the railroad along the north bank of the Columbia.

In 1905 Hidden's sons took over his brick business and installed a machine to replace the hand system. It was to be expected that they would have brick houses of their own. W. Foster Hidden's at 13th and Washington Streets, built in 1913, is the upper one on the preceding page.

A mansard roof with arched windows in it was a rarity. Charles Brown, founder of the First National Bank of Vancouver, built this one on his dwelling at 400 West Eleventh Street. The house has other interesting architectural details, such as the porch railing, the paired brackets under the eaves and the decoration at the top of the posts.

The home was erected in the late 1880's when Brown's was the only banking facility in town. Like many other financial institutions, it suffered in the 1893 depression and was forced to close its doors in 1901 as a consequence of losses on loans. Both Brown and his cashier committed suicide when the bank failed. Mrs. Brown continued to reside in the house until her death in 1910.

It is recalled about the family that Samuel Brown, Charles' father, was a former mayor of Galesburg, Ill. and had presided at the Lincoln-Douglas debate in that city. A personal friendship with Lincoln resulted and Samuel Brown in 1861 was appointed receiver of the Vancouver branch of the General Land Office.

James R. Gregg, attorney, is the current occupant of the house.

The Jackson Inn on the military road two miles west of Castle Rock lately has undergone remodelling. The front porch has been removed, two door openings have been closed and a new one created. Perhaps this makes for better living inside, but for the purposes of making a picture it is a photogenic disaster. Only the wide eaves, returned cornices and small window panes suggest the former classical lines.

Henry and Elizabeth Jackson, first occupants of the house, journeyed west by wagon train from Illinois bringing their younger children. Their eldest daughter had migrated to Oregon Territory in its earliest years as wife of a missionary, but was killed when thrown from a horse.

The Jacksons took up a 320-acre donation claim and their eldest son took another. They were all together in the wagon train and built log cabins within sight of each other. During the Indian trouble they spent some time in a community blockhouse. The son's family returned home, dug a cave nearby and stayed in it at night.

In 1857 Henry Jackson began his new home, intending it as a wayside inn for stagecoach and

wagon travelers. One front door led to the ladies' parlor, the other was for the men's room. Between the two was a double fireplace. The kitchen and utilitarian rooms were in a lean-to at the back. John Burbee, a cabinetmaker who married Henry's youngest daughter, Amanda, made much of the furniture for the inn at his workshop.

Regular stages ran between Monticello (present Longview) and Puget Sound and the company contracted with the Jacksons to board passengers and stable extra teams. The old barn where stage horses were kept collapsed in 1930 during a heavy snow fall.

After Elizabeth Jackson died Henry married the widow of Jonathan Burbee. They moved to Freeport and Bill and Mary Jackson stayed on as owners of the inn. Employing ox teams, they turned the house from its position facing west, so that it faced north. They tore down the lean-to and added an ell which contained a large dining room and kitchen. The upstairs of the new part never was finished, but served for dances, elections and public meetings. The rear wing featured in this view, has again been remodelled.

In 1872 the Northern Pacific Railroad was completed from Kalama to Olequa and stages ceased to travel the road past the country inn.

Present occupants of the house gave to the Cowlitz County Museum doors, paneling, window frames, a fireplace and other materials for recreating the ladies' parlor. It now fills a small room at the southwest corner of the museum in Kelso.

Joseph Borst was of Dutch ancestry, born in 1821 in New York state. He crossed the plains in 1845 and in 1854 he married 16-year-old Mary Adeline Roundtree, one of the first white girls on Grays Harbor, later of Boisfort.

Early in their married life, with their six-weeks-old baby, they had taken refuge from the Indians in Fort Henness. They were there frequently both in the fall of 1855 and the following spring. During that spring a company of 30 soldiers built a storage depot at the forks of the Skookumchuck and the Chehalis Rivers, where Borst had taken a donation claim. Borst helped haul logs for the structure.

He had a small cabin nearby, but his wife made him promise some day to build her a new white house. He must have enlarged the cabin, for in the fall of 1856 it was described as a long, low house of logs and shakes, with three rooms and an attic.

After the couple's return from Fort Henness Borst rented his farm for a time. Meanwhile he purchased the storehouse from the government for $500. He cut doors and windows in it and made a hole for a chimney and moved his family in. His second daughter was born in a room on the second floor, Joseph delivering the child.

In a little over ten years after her marriage Mary Adeline had her big white house with green shutters, a veranda and an upper balcony. It had taken almost two years to build, Joseph insisting upon a thorough job. The ends of every board were dipped in white lead to waterproof the joints. The house was of solid studding construction, with wooden

pegs used as nails. Castings and hardware were shipped from San Francisco and the lumber was hauled from Tumwater and dried. A German carpenter, Jake Ort, did the construction and a Dane painted and grained the woodwork. At first the walls were lined with muslin and whitewashed; plaster and paper came later. A large soapstone fireplace was built in the dining room; a cook stove was brought around the Horn. The furniture was handmade by a man on Chambers Prairie. It included six maple spool beds with ropes across the frames, straw mattresses and feather beds.

The Borsts did everything in style. Since they had a large family a teacher lived in the house with them and conducted school.

Altogether the Borsts had a regular community of their own, consisting of the blockhouse, the old home, and old store building and a huge barn. Between the residence and the blockhouse on the river bank Borst operated a ferry which carried travelers on the military road across the Chehalis.

Charles Gilchrist, a native of Scotland, seemed to prosper in everything he attempted. He came to Washington in 1878 after making a fortune out of lumber at Washoe, Nevada. He purchased a small mill at Centralia and not so long afterward founded the Lewis County Bank.

He built this house about 1886 and it became the talk of the town because of the skylight in the top of the third story, where the owner had a billiard room. Beneath this odd-looking lighting arrangement Gilchrist had his billiard table and enjoyed many a game with business associates.

The skylight was badly damaged during the Columbus Day storm of 1962 and, suitable materials not being available to restore some of the windows, makeshift repairs had to be made.

One might pass the house of Noah B. Coffman, Chehalis banker, as being unexceptional, but it would be hard to dismiss his barn, for it is among the most unusual in the state. The structures were built within two years of each other, the house in 1900, the barn in 1902.

Coffman, of Pennsylvania German ancestry, was born in Indiana in 1857. He went to Tacoma as a bank cashier during the boom days of 1883. After going east to marry, he wanted to settle in an agricultural district and chose Chehalis, where for a time he was in an insurance, real estate and commercial law office. Finding the town had need of a bank, he made a small beginning and organized a private bank with a partner, J. M. Allen, in 1884. This became the Coffman, Dobson & Co. bank. Coffman retired in 1932 after 48 years of service with the firm and continued his connection with it until his death in 1940.

With his associates Coffman platted and sold most of Chehalis. He gave his personal attention to dairying and built up a Jersey herd. His barn was noted as one of the finest in Washington. Here he and his son conducted a model dairy on their home property.

The barn is owned now by Mr. and Mrs. Don Bliss, of 905 St. Helens Avenue. The brick house is at 899 St. Helens Avenue.

Montesano

Now a funeral home, this was the last residence of Charles N. Byles, who platted the townsite of Montesano, first settlement north of the Chehalis River. He was a member of the 1853 wagon train which made history by crossing through Naches Pass.

Byles was the son of a pioneer minister. The youth left the family farm to obtain an education, worked his way in schools and was graduated from a Portland business college. He was appointed United States land surveyor and with a brother did much surveying in Western Washington.

Each winter Charles taught school for three months. In 1870 he invested his earnings in the J. N. King land claim on which he later platted the town. That same year he married Eliza Medcalf, who was Montesano's first woman teacher.

Byles was county auditor, county treasurer, mayor and organizer of the first bank. In 1886 he donated land on which to build the court house.

After Byles' death the residence at 121 Broadway W. was for many years the home of C. O. Durdle, dairyman. Its present owner is Perry McDonald.

As the front of this pale green residence at 111 First Avenue N., Montesano was in the shadow, the photographer snapped a rear view of the house, built in the 1880's. It has been moved from an earlier location and undergone some modernizing.

Judge Mason Irwin of the superior court was its first occupant. He was from Pennsylvania and grew up on a farm. While working in a bank he began reading law and was admitted to the bar in 1879 when he was 29 years of age. Although he was elected prosecuting attorney of his home county, he was determined to go west. He arrived in Montesano in 1885, at first engaging in private practice. He was elected to the judgeship in 1889 and was married in 1894. The couple had five children, who grew up in the comfortable home.

With a larger front porch and the massive side bay windows unconcealed by shrubbery, this was in 1890 rated the handsomest residence anywhere within many miles of Montesano. It was completed in August, 1889 at a cost of $4,500. Its dimensions were 32 by 41½ feet, on grounds 120 by 250 feet. The house at 310 Broadway East had 12 rooms and was pleasantly situated on a knoll commanding a view of the town.

The mansion belonged to Lewis E. Bignold, a native of England who emigrated to the United States in 1873. He studied law in Nebraska and was admitted to the bar in that state. He moved to Montesano in 1883 and became one of the town's most prominent citizens, first its city attorney and then in 1885 its mayor.

A story is told of how the house narrowly escaped damage during commemoration of the 100th anniversary of the inauguration of George Washington as President. Appropriate exercises were being held at a large gathering in the center of the village and a man was designated to fire a cannon in honor of the occasion. He did so successfully several times, then put in an extra heavy load and the weapon exploded. A 15-pound piece of iron sailed up in the air, was carried several blocks and burried itself 18 inches deep in Bignold's yard. Fortunately no one was injured.

Bright yellow paint gives a fresh look to the former James W. Divilbiss home at 134 Fleet Street, upper right. He was editor and publisher of The Vidette, Grays Harbor County's oldest newspaper. It was founded in 1882 and Divilbiss was its third owner, acquiring it in 1887 when he just had arrived from Kansas and was experiencing his initial venture into journalism.

Montesano's public library is named for William H. Abel, who erected the lower house, 117 Fleet Street, early in the present century. He was born in Sussex, England in 1870 and moved to Montesano when he was 22. He was admitted to the bar two years later, having graduated from the University of Kansas law school.

Abel became famed as one of Washington's leading trial and defense lawyers. His best known case was that centered around the I.W.W. trials following the 1919 Armistice Day massacre in Centralia.

The attorney was a great book lover and at one time owned 15,000 volumes. He gave books generously to schools and to Grays Harbor County.

Mrs. James Cooney's residence at 130 N. Main Street, Montesano, is an example of the use of fancy shingles. The house (page 128) was built in 1909 for George Hubble, tugboat operator, who had an earlier dwelling on the corner. He moved this to the right of the property and it is presently the office of Dr. Lester McCracken. The older dwelling dates from 1890.

Hubble had a taste for elaborate decoration both in the jigsaw trim of his earlier home and in the shingles and murals of his later one. George Tal-

bott, the carpenter in charge of building the larger house, expended great effort on the interior. The woodwork was put together with brass screws, there are carved balusters on the stairs and the fireplace is of mahogany with bookcases built alongside. The cove ceilings in the principal rooms have a frieze of varying scenes from the Rhineland and Bavaria. Lighting fixtures are of prism type from Czecho Slovakia.

Mrs. Cooney has preserved the original decor, a fitting setting for her many antique furnishings.

The **Albert Schafer mansion** in Montesano sold in 1967 for $10. There was only one bidder. He was allowed six months in which to move the structure from property between the court house and the city hall which the Schafer heirs had given to the municipality.

The house, shown below, was completed in 1911, just prior to the marriage of Schafer and Helen Carothers. It was remodelled in the late 1920's, when a garden, pool and tennis court were developed.

As it stood on its original site the home had four floors, a green house and servants' quarters. It boasted five bath rooms.

Schafer was one of three brothers born on a farm in the Satsop Valley of German parents, who had moved there in 1870. The brothers logged by ox team on the family lands and built a timber empire of their own. At the peak of their operations they had two sawmills and a shingle mill in Montesano, another sawmill and a shingle mill in Aberdeen, a sawmill at Dryad, a logging railroad and a steamship line.

Albert Schafer lived in his house until his death in 1945 and his wife stayed on until she died in 1964.

Grays Harbor

Without doubt the most imposing landmark at Ocosta, in Grays Harbor County, is this relic of the boom days, when the community was to have become a Northern Pacific Railroad terminal.

The mansion was built in 1892 for Robert Boyle, a leading citizen when Ocosta-by-the-Sea was flourishing. The place began as Bay City in 1884, but when the Northern Pacific was about to complete its auxiliary line from the coast to Tacoma a great fanfare of publicity developed about the proposed port and it was given a new name. On May 1, 1890 an excursion of over 1,000 persons went there and 300 lots were sold. By 1892 Ocosta had a sawmill, sash and door factory, brewery, flour mill, three shingle mills, logging camps and fisheries and was negotiating for a clam cannery. The large frame, four-story McCandless Hotel had been built, streets were planked and the population was 800.

The price of a lot in the business district had reached as high as $6,500 before the panic of 1893 wiped out the burgeoning metropolis. Meanwhile Aberdeen citizens laid a mile of track to connect with Grays Harbor Junction and caused the railroad to abandon its plan to make Ocosta the terminal. The rails were torn up, the planked street and sidewalks were left to rot and the long dock fell in ruins.

Ocosta never had a chance of reviving. Its shipping facilities were poor, the harbor was shallow and log booms anchored there broke up in gales. By 1932 the population dwindled to 80 registered voters and it was decided to disincorporate.

John Grossman has lived in the Boyle house since 1903. When his parents took it over deterioration had set in and much restorative work was needed.

In 1949 Grossman was wrecking a barn on the ranch (the barn had originally been a church) and found a prospectus of Ocosta printed in 1890. It showed carriages dashing through the streets, sailing ships at anchor, mills surrounded by high-piled lumber and an 11-car railroad train on the track.

By the Grossmans' day Ocosta already had reverted to tall grass and a few ruins where buildings had stood.

Josiah O. Stearns built this about 1890 at the southwest corner of 10th and K. Streets, Hoquiam, the residence was then close to the Northwestern Lumber Co. mill. No railroad was near it, as now. The ground tended to be marshy and the foundations rested on piling.

Stearns was a young bachelor who had inherited logging interests and railroad bonds. He was fond of social life and his home was the scene of parties and was loaned to friends for weddings. Now it is to become a mortuary.

The house, on a large corner lot, is among Hoquiam's oldest structures. Of interest is the octagonal tower with port holes. An arched stained glass window can be seen.

Here is an extreme example of the use of fancy-butt shingles on a home at 1715 Riverside Drive, Hoquiam, built by George L. Davis, a logger, in the 1890's. His logging show was in the vicinity of New London.

In that period the shingles often did not come from Washington sources, but were brought to Grays Harbor from redwood mills in California in the holds of lumber schooners.

This house recently has been owned by Dr. Howard Bryant.

Against a hillside on Chenault Street in Hoquiam stand the homes of two brothers, Joseph (left) and Robert Lytle, built in the 1890's when turrets and stained glass were the mode.

The Lytle brothers started their fortunes as grocers in the first year of that decade and through this business they outfitted small logging companies. Some went broke and left the brothers holding liens against their equipment. Thus the firm evolved into the Lytle Mercantile and Logging Co., which successfully carried on timber operations in two locales. By 1911 it had logging railroads at Porter and at the head of tidewater on the East Hoquiam River and employed 300 men.

In 1899 the three-story Lytle Brothers Block was completed and the top floor was rented by the Hoquiam Commercial Club. The grocery was in part of the ground floor.

Aberdeen has a Swiss chalet built entirely of cedar. It stands at 712 North Broadway and is among the city's oldest homes, having been erected in 1908 for John B. Elston. He was one of the boom-time business men in Ocosta, who left after the bubble burst and became associated with the grocery business in Aberdeen.

When Elston decided to build he went to the American Mill Co. to order the cedar lumber, but B. J. Johnson, the owner, refused and told him to go somewhere else. All of the local mills turned down the request because they were not sawing cedar. Elston returned to Johnson, who said all right, he would furnish the order, but it would cost $35 a thousand feet, an unheard-of-price at that time.

Young Ray Johnson had the job of delivering the lumber by team up the steep hill. The road was full of stumps, the mud was slippery and the boards were inclined to slide off the load. The youth never felt kindly about Elston's taste for cedar because of the bad time Ray had getting the lumber to the site.

Since it was built the chalet has been altered and had additions. Its present owner is Dr. Budnick.

Trees nearly conceal this house Jerry McGillicuddy built in Aberdeen in 1902. It is at the corner of L and Eighth Streets and represents the city's older types of houses. Note the oblong pattern of the frieze and the numerous brackets of the eaves.

McGillicuddy always was a lumberman though he engaged at times in other sorts of business such as real estate and loans. He lived at different periods in Montesano and Hoquiam but finally settled in Aberdeen, where he specialized in timber cruising. Some of his sons followed their father's footsteps and the 1907 city directory listed three McGillicuddys as timber cruisers, all living under this same roof.

Almerion Stockwell, who was in investments and timber lands in Aberdeen early in the present century, built this handsome residence about 1909 at 102 E. Eighth Street. It is now owned by Gene Whiteside, mortician, who purchased it in 1920.

The hitching post in the front yard is a reminder of the days before there were automobiles and the house had a large barn. The figure now carries a lantern to light the flight of steps from the street.

Remarkable on this otherwise severe residence at 122 Fifth Avenue W., Aberdeen are the curved panes of the bay window. The house was erected early in the century by Mr. Schutt of the Grays Harbor Logging Co.

Colonial columns dignify this Aberdeen house at 119 N. Broadway, built in 1907 by Frank Hawks.

One wanted servants to wash window panes like these in the George Hopkins home at 1005 N. Broadway, Aberdeen. The house was erected in 1909. Hopkins inherited much land from his father and retained an entire block of it when he built. Some of the grounds have since been sold.

Curved glass panes are in this turret and the window below it at 619 First Street N., Aberdeen. Towers were still in fashion in 1908 when a Mr. Anderson built this home, but they would soon be on the way out except in the manor-house type of dwelling.

Whatcom County

This Bellingham home is known as Jim Wardner's castle.

Wardner was born in Milwaukee, Wis. in 1846. He spent 62 years wandering around following the goddess of fortune where pastures looked most green. Invariably he turned up broke at some new mining camp.

He was a self advertiser and diplomat, very shrewd and with expansive ideas. He made more than $100,000 at the Bunker-Hill-Sullivan silver-lead mine near Wardner, Idaho. He was not its locator, but was so soon on the ground he secured water rights, which the discoverers had overlooked. The best mine on earth could prove worthless without water, so this brought him a partnership and he put the mine on the map.

It happened that 1889 was a bad year for him. He had heavy losses on wheat and oil stocks and about this time he met Nelson Bennett, who was endeavoring to promote Fairhaven on Bellingham Bay as a metropolis. Bennett talked Wardner into getting in on the ground floor. The latter bought 135 lots, organized the water works, an electric company, the Samish Lake Logging & Milling Co. and the Fairhaven National Bank. He was either president or vice president of all of these. He cleaned up $60,000 from real estate in 60 days and bought the Blue Canyon coal mine.

By January, 1890 Wardner was building the castle on Wardner Hill and a few months later he was causing a sensation by proposing to start a black cat fur farm on Eliza Island, which he could see out in the harbor, not far from his imposing home.

The next year he sold his coal mine to a group of Montana capitalists.

Money was getting tight and Wardner was caught in the squeeze when the panic of 1893 caused him heavy losses. He liquidated his Fairhaven holdings and made a trip to South Africa, expecting to recoup his finances. This did not prove a profitable step. He went next to British Columbia, where he founded Wardner, B. C., the second town to bear his name. Then he went to Alaska and finally to Mexico, each time expecting to promote mines. He died on the way home from the last place.

Wherever he lived in this country his name became a legend. His house overlooking Fairhaven still is associated with him, though he owned it only briefly.

When Fairhaven was riding its wave of prosperity as an independent community on Bellingham Bay, the outstanding firm of local architects was Longstaff & Black, both from Boston.

Frank Longstaff designed this residence for himself and built it at 1210 Gambier Street on the slope overlooking Fairhaven soon after moving west in the summer of 1890. He had been engaged to build the Fairhaven Hotel. That fall he sent for his partner and they were kept busy with such structures as the Sisters Hospital, Jim Wardner's and many other residences. Soon H. N. Black was attending to all of the office work and Longstaff took over outside supervision of their projects.

Black and Longstaff shared the new home. Like most of their designs, it had to have a turret. This is a modest one compared with some, but inasmuch as it faced the harbor, its windows took in a magnificent view.

Henry Bateman's mansion at 15th and Knox Avenue in Bellingham is another relic of the glory days of Fairhaven. Bateman was employed in the big Hotel Fairhaven, built by Dan Harris, and later was in business for himself. The house, all-over spindles and fancy millwork, dates from about 1890.

Among stately mansions of the 1890's Roland Greene Gamwell's Bellingham home had few equals in Washington. The structure was as expansive as its owner's plans to make Fairhaven, on the south shore of Bellingham Bay "the imperial city of the West." Gamwell, the moving spirit of the Fairhaven Land Co. expected to see his town become the rail terminal metropolis of the Northwest.

He built the mansion for his Boston bride, Helen Thacher Gamwell, engaging the services of Longstaff and Black, the architects whom he had employed to design his Fairhaven Hotel. The house, at 1001 16th Street, required two years to build. Most time-consuming was the carving of a solid oak staircase by Italian artisans from Seattle. The dwelling was ready for occupancy in July, 1892, complete with silver, china and linens brought from the East Coast.

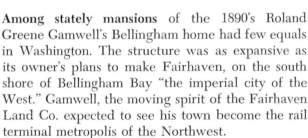

Gamwell lived in the house nearly 67 years. Some of his furnishings are still there—a gold leaf mirror, towering mahogany dragon's foot bookcase, the dining room suite, Oriental rugs, needlepoint chairs and some heavy bed room pieces.

Rooms set a new fashion for spaciousness in Bellingham, for there are only nine main ones in the great house. The garden was extensive and was the scene of outdoor parties. The entrance hall was large enough for dancing, while the musicians were accommodated in space beneath the huge curve of the stairs.

Gamwell, a native of Providence, R.I., was an engineering graduate of Massachusetts Institute of Technology who came out to the West to reroute the interurban transportation system of Tacoma. There he met Nelson Bennett, the millionaire contractor who was promoting Fairhaven, and went to Bellingham Bay in 1889. After collapse of the railroad boom Gamwell stayed on and engaged in successful business enterprises. Among celebrities he entertained in his home were Samuel C. Clemens and President William Howard Taft.

Gamwell had a large personal library, was a devotee of whist and raised rare roses. He lived on alone in the house after his wife's death in 1944. He died in 1959.

The present owner is Mrs. Wilfred E. Vostli, librarian at Western Washington State College.

Dr. Charles Welch of Ferndale built this house with modified mansard roof and sold in 1909 to Dr. Gerald Roy Bice, who took over the former's practice. About three years later Dr. Bice remodelled the dwelling.

Dr. Bice died in 1933 but his widow continued to live there another 20 years.

The Bices were from Iowa. They were active in civic affairs and he served several terms as mayor. Mrs. Bice organized Ferndale's first Parent Teacher Association. She worked for the State Department of Public Assistance until her retirement at the age of 72.

The doctor kept his horses in a barn behind the house and a niece recalls the fun of climbing around and playing there.

Skagit County

Dr. T. B. Childs, Anacortes pioneer and the town's first postmaster, built the house, upper right, in 1891. His daughter, Mrs. Marian Childs Watkinson, lived there until she died two years ago.

Mrs. Childs was a sister of Anna Curtis Bowman, from whom Anacortes derived its name. Her husband, Amos Bowman, founded the settlement.

Dr. Childs was fond of beautiful woods and it is reported that the house contained 48 different kinds brought from Brazil. The wainscoting in the dining room is of alternating panels of redwood and cedar. In a corner of the entrance hall is a rosewood fireplace and another is in the library, with a bronze grate. Ceilings are 12 feet and some have moldings in gold leaf. The main stairway has elegantly carved newel posts.

Most of the furniture was still in the house when Mrs. Watkinson's estate was settled, among the pieces being an ebony piano that was brought around Cape Horn in 1897.

The carriage house is still intact and has a trim of colored glass around the entry.

City Manager Earl Diller of Anacortes lives at 1201 Fifth Avenue in a residence generally associated with Captain John A. Matheson, a native of Nova Scotia who owned Bering Sea codfish boats and was a fish packer.

The house had an earlier owner named McDonald, but it was smaller then. Captain Matheson added all of the right-hand portion.

Matheson sent his boat, the *Lizzie Colby*, around Cape Horn in 1890 while he traveled overland and established the Pacific Coast's first codfish plant at the foot of K Avenue in Anacortes. An old newspaper clipping tells of the *Lizzie* coming in "like a great swan," laden with fish after its summer season in the North in 1891.

This was known as the Captain Hogan house, built in 1891 at 1613 Seventh Avenue by Anacortes' first mayor. He never married and was remembered as a well dressed gentleman in high hat and carrying a cane. He built two other houses at Fifth and M Streets, which later were moved. This, his original residence, was sold to Doug Allmond, who owned the city's light plant.

From notes supplied by Mrs. Douglas Bullock Kimsey we learned that F. V. Hogan was born in 1842 in Bastrop County, Texas, attended a military academy and served in the Confederate Army until the close of the war, coming out a major. He was in mercantile business and in real estate in Texas before going to California in 1880. Eight years later he moved to Tacoma and in 1889 became interested in buying Anacortes property and promoting the town.

He organized a new company, Hogan and Hagen, in 1891 and handled all of the Anacortes interests of the Oregon Improvement Co. His partner had been identified with the latter firm previously at Port Townsend.

The Arthur P. Sharpstein house at 32nd Street and M Avenue in Anacortes belongs to the railroad boom period when every coastal town aspired to become a terminal port.

Again we are indebted to Mrs. Kimsey for her research on this early citizen. A native of Wisconsin, Sharpstein moved to Walla Walla with his parents in 1860. After going East to complete his education, he returned to Walla Walla and engaged in journalism, becoming city editor successively of three different newspapers. By 1884 he turned to law, studying in San Francisco. In the fall of that year he was appointed United States commissioner to the New Orleans Exposition.

His law practice carried him to Pendleton, Ore. and to the Coeur d'Alenes. He made considerable money from his profession and from mining interests, among them the Roslyn coalfields. He invested in Anacortes property in 1889 and was astute at pyramiding a small amount of capital into a large section of real estate.

That same year Sharpstein married and erected his stately home. Many families have lived in it since, among the best remembered being Mr. and Mrs. William T. Odlin, parents of Reno Odlin. Both father and son became prominent in the banking field, moving later to Tacoma.

Reno Odlin remembers that the house seemed very far out. During the worst winter months the family would move into Anacortes and occupy quarters in the home of friends. An arrangement was made to take meals in a restaurant.

"Even after Dad got a car, a two-cylinder Reo," Odlin said, "the trip out Commercial Avenue to 32nd Street and then up the little hill four or five blocks to M Street was really quite a safari. So we continued to spend a couple of winter months downtown. Then they filled in some of the chuck holes and gravelled Commercial Avenue and Dad got a better car, a four-cylinder Hudson. From that time on we didn't move into the city because we could get home. Mother loved the old house and they lived there until after Dad's retirement."

Mrs. Guy F. Simpson, who lives in this house at 904 32nd Street, Anacortes, says it was built by Henry Howard in the 1880's. It had seven lots with it. Howard may have logged, fished or farmed, or done all three. He was so far out from town he had to go through tall timber to his nearest neighbor. To get supplies he brought them up Fidalgo Bay by boat and carried them in over a trail from the waterfront. Now the city has grown all around his place.

The Simpsons bought the house in 1921 and did some remodelling. Formerly the front entrance looked toward the water and there was a porch across that side of the building.

Most of the old window panes are still in the home.

Painted a bright light blue, the old home of Skagit Valley pioneer Mike Sullivan stands on the fertile delta about a mile north of LaConner. Sullivan was among the first to dike land for a farm in that region. He lived in a smaller home until about 1890 when everybody who could afford it was going into something more ornate and spacious.

His farm boasted an isolated grove of juniper trees, which the children roundabout termed "red cedar." For this reason Sullivan called his new farmhouse Cedar Grove, to match that of his neighbor, John Conner, who had Clover Lawn. The grove was a popular place for picnics. Several of the junipers are standing, but most of the trees around the house are more recent plantings of other species.

The Sullivan farm grew crops of oats and hay in early years. River boats used to go up Sullivan's Slough to load shipments for Seattle, as the slough was navigable to the farm.

About 1883, perhaps a little later, George Gasches, LaConner merchant, erected this big dwelling, now known as the Castle Apartments. About 1915 it was for a time the Skagit Valley Hospital.

Large slabs of granite rock, ferried down the Skagit River, were used for the foundation, laid by a skilled rock mason. Heavy timbers were cheap in those days, so the joists and beams underneath the building are remarkable for their size and strength. The house had 22 rooms and three fireplaces. It has been converted into apartments since 1940.

Edward Good purchased this 160-acre farm west of Conway early in the 1870's and in 1904 hired a German carpenter to build the substantial home that now occupies an attractive rural setting. The man was an old-country craftsman who spared no effort and used quality materials. The shingle roof lasted 60 years.

Good was from New Brunswick and brought the idea of a widow's walk from the Canadian maritime provinces.

The rooms are large and most have bay windows with excellent views of Mount Baker, the Olympics and, on clear days, Mount Rainier.

Ownership was out of the family for a few years, but in 1935 Good's granddaughter and her husband, Mr. and Mrs. Lowell Hughes, bought the place. They modernized the residence slightly before moving in and, again 13 years later, did some remodeling. The exterior remains almost exactly as it was in

Good's day, except for the addition of a fireplace.

Years ago a good size slough, a branch of the Skagit River, flowed near the front yard and Indians passed frequently in their canoes en route to the tide flats to dig clams.

Easily the most striking dwelling in the vicinity of Lyman, Skagit County, is the former home of B. D. Minkler at 129 Main Street. It was erected in 1891 and the plain posts across the front were replaced later with stately columns. The sunburst trim is part of the original decor.

Minkler was the pioneer mill man in the Upper Skagit Valley. Around 1880 he established the first sawmill at Birdsview, a place he named for himself. Since he was Bird Minkler, when he had to call his post office something, he thought Birdsview an appropriate designation.

Leaving that community, he bought a general merchandise store in Lyman and founded the Lyman Lumber and Shingle Co. He was active in politics and served in the first House of Representatives when Washington became a state. Later he was in the Senate.

V. E. Field, who has lived in the house at Lyman since 1954, married Minkler's granddaughter.

Snohomish County

At upper right is one of Snohomish's oldest houses, built in 1880 when the town was beginning to boom. The quarter block at 1012 Fourth Street was then almost in the woods.

W. M. Snyder, Sr. was the first and long-time owner. He came from Galena, Ill., where he had been a banker, a profession he followed in Snohomish. He erected the house soon after his arrival.

This side view looks quite different from the original. Formerly the gables had diamond-shaped windows centering a board trim laid in diamond pattern. The owner facetiously referred to it as "North Dakota Renaissance." As first constructed the back part of the home consisted of a pump house and cow barn, but alterations and additions were made so frequently that this structure was soon replaced with an entire rear wing. Incidentally, the family cow used to be turned out to graze in the surrounding stump land.

A feature at the big double front doors was a vestibule with storm door, a holdover from Snyder's experience with cold weather in the Middle West. There are still many colored window panes in the rooms. Others removed during alterations were found stacked in the attic when McLean Snyder, the son, sold the place.

Four fireplaces and a winding staircase are intact. The interesting porch railing is exactly as it was when first built.

Willis Tucker is present owner of the residence.

When Mr. and Mrs. Arthur Ashcraft purchased this attractive residence at 329 Avenue C, Snohomish in 1957 it hadn't received a new coat of paint in 30 years and was in poor condition. The Ashcrafts like rehabilitating old homes, so they took to this one with gusto and have successfully restored it.

The original owner was Judge W. P. Bell, the attorney who handled the incorporation of Snohomish in 1888. The house dates from 1892.

An unusual feature is a chimney with three fireplaces on the main floor, back to back in triangular fashion in the living room, dining room and entrance hall. The main doorway is in the porch at the right hand side, below two windows which light the carved oak staircase. The porch extends on three side of the house.

Doors and all of the interior woodwork are of western red cedar. Evidently this wood was cut and made up in Snohomish, where cedar abounded.

Ashcraft said that values fell so low during depression years that the house and two lots sold for less than the property itself originally cost.

With its spindlework and colored glass bordering the windows, this Snohomish residence cost only $2,000 in 1890 when Samuel Vestal had it built. He was one of the organizers of the Snohomish First National Bank and for 40 years a director. He was a member of the first state senate. Vestal served as county treasurer and county auditor and at the time of his death in 1927 was city treasurer.

Mrs. Vestal was of earlier pioneer stock than her husband. Her father, Norman Martin, was a Scotch carpenter who came to Washington in 1843 to work for the Hudson's Bay Co. and her mother crossed the plains in 1847.

The Vestals were married in 1877 in Kalama, where he was a merchant and also county treasurer. After moving to Snohomish in 1884 they needed a big house, for they had eight children.

The residence remained in the family until 1967.

The present Roy Marler residence at 430 Avenue B in Snohomish, built by V. K. Loose, banker and promoter, is another souvenir of the boom-and-bust period of the early 1890's. Loose was with the Snohomish National Bank and, when it failed, went to Seattle. B. F. Bird of the Cascade mill lived in the place later.

The house, upper right, is notable for the spindle trim and curving portion of its porch. Some of the windows are intricately inlaid with small panes.

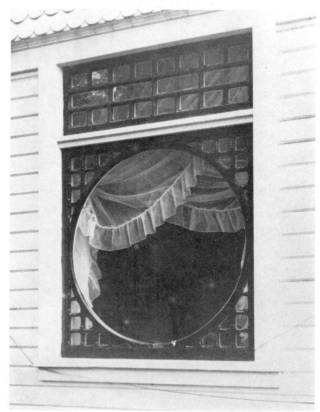

The Snohomish residence below, at 506 Avenue B, was erected in 1902 for George T. Hendrie, pharmacist. The front porch has been greatly altered. The house reflects the workmanship of Nels Peter Hansen, carpenter and builder who is remembered by old timers. He was a Dane who arrived in Snohomish in 1884 and built many of the best homes. Traces of his craftsmanship are to be seen in the or-namental trim under the bay windows and across the center, also the finely finished stairway between floors.

Mr. and Mrs. Harold King purchased the residence in 1956 and remodeled it. They are proud of a large tree with edible chestnuts in one corner of the yard. Hendrie brought the seedling all the way from his native New Hampshire.

The proprietors of an antique shop scarcely could have found a more appropriate spot than Stanwood's Heritage House, once the home of D. O. Pearson. Appropriately, it stands on Pearson Street, at Market. Architectural features are its mansard roof with gables, two friezes of fancy-butt shingles, a bay window with a second-floor extension and two circular porthole windows above the front door.

The Pearsons were leading citizens of the town, the husband its first mayor and owner of its oldest retail store, and the wife, Clara Stanwood Pearson, whose maiden name was given to the community. Pearson arrived in Stanwood from Massachusetts and opened his first store when the place was called Centerville and consisted of several shacks along the waterfront. He ministered to all sorts of needs of settlers and Indians, was their lawyer, tooth extractor, amateur doctor and postmaster as well as merchant.

The door and hitching post are recent embellishments by the present occupants, but the fancy shinglework was there when the house was new.

Seattle

This is the oldest house in Seattle, supposed to have been erected by Dr. David S. Maynard in 1854. Other sources say it was built between 1857 and 1862 and might have been put up by N. S. Kellogg, who for 11 months owned the property on which it stood before the land reverted back to Maynard.

The residence, formerly at 64th and Alki Avenue, is now at 3045 64th Avenue S.W. It was on beach property which Charles C. Terry sold in 1857 to Dr. Maynard. The next permanent owner was Hans Hansen, a native of Norway, who married in Wisconsin and crossed the plains with his bride in 1866. The couple arrived at Alki Point three years later and took over Maynard's house. Hansen logged, had an interest in a brick company and, in the 1890's, rented camp sites to summer vacationers visiting Alki.

Today the house looks very different from its appearance before being moved in 1915. It once had a large lean-to section on the right hand side, similar to the one on the left. As originally built, it had nine rooms and was heated by two fireplaces and a cook stove. The arrangement of windows then consisted of pairs of singles upstairs and downstairs, all with small panes.

Sandwiched between two buildings on Boren Avenue, just south of Pike Street in Seattle is a remnant of the 1880's. It was once surrounded by lawn and was centered on half of a city block.

The house was bult by Mr. and Mrs. George W. Ward. He was in the insurance, real estate and loan business and was prominently identified with a Japanese Baptist mission, helping to found it and taking part in its activities for 26 years.

The couple purchased the property for their new house in 1883 and lived there until shortly after the financial panic ten years later. After it was given

up, the house passed through the hands of several real-estate men and about 1905 the property was sold for hotel development. To make way for a brick structure, now the Crest Hotel on Pike Street, the house was turned crosswise on the lot so that it fronted on Boren. It was divided into accommodations for eight lodgers and became an annex to the hotel.

Among the houses always considered worth saving in Seattle is the one at 421 30th Avenue South which Judge James T. Ronald remodelled in 1889 from a simple five-room dwelling. He had then been living in the city seven years, engaging in a law practice with Samuel Piles, who became United States senator. It was a successful combination and, as Ronald was active in organizing the first Democratic club in the city, he was rewarded with the post of prosecuting attorney from 1885 to 1889. Next year he was elected mayor and served to 1894.

When Ronald purchased the property on 30th Avenue, Seattle just had gone through its great and devastating fire. The rising politician needed a suitable home and, being brought up amid Southern traditions, he hired an architect from Virginia to re-model the little house he had purchased. The judge spent $30,000 on the reconstruction and the results were impressive.

A living room, 36 feet long, took up an entire side of the residence. The second floor at one side had a circular porch, reached through French doors from two bed rooms. There were six bed rooms altogether and an enormous attic with an arched window.

Four stately columns across the front, many small bevelled glass window panes and a library finished with a frieze of hunting scenes were distinctive features.

Lately the spacious structure has been made over into Ronald Hall, a halfway house operated as a social agency where probationers, parolees and some transient men stay.

The Jefferson Park Ladies Club at 2336 15th Avenue S., Seattle occupies the first house built on Beacon Hill. It was a private home, erected in 1886, and for a long time stood in the midst of a pear orchard.

The club purchased the house in 1915 and added the wing at the left. The club's purpose was to spearhead improvements needed on the hill. As organizations go, it is one of the oldest in Seattle.

Seattle's Men's University Club occupies quarters which are really two residences put together. The main part, to the left, was erected by Martin Van Buren Stacy about 1889 or slightly earlier.

Keeping track of the Stacy residences would require a special researcher's services, for this pioneer capitalist and his wife got along none too well and they moved in and out of homes almost on a stand-by basis. If Martin was at one address, his fiery wife generally was at another.

First the couple built a French style (Third Empire) wooden mansion on Marion Street (long a part of Blanc's Cafe), but they did not move in and it stood empty several years. Instead of furnishing it they went into the house near the corner of Boren and Madison Streets, because Mrs. Stacy wished to be close to a friend who lived in the same vicinity. Mrs. Stacy was wealthy in her own right and went on building other houses in the neighborhood. By 1891 the city directory shows that her husband was living in a hotel—maybe Mrs. Stacy went on residing in the Boren Avenue house. In 1893 Senator Cyrus F. Clapp was renting it furnished and by that time Mrs. Stacy refused to set foot in the place. In

1901 Lyman Colt bought it and soon sold to the club.

Stacy died in 1901 and his wife passed away three years later. They had no children.

The club added wings to the residence, closed up some fireplaces and made many interior changes.

When new in the early 1890's Captain William R. Ballard's house at the northwest corner of Columbia and Minor Avenue was painted a fashionable red. It had a barn and at one side a croquet lawn. The finest feature of the home was its bay window over the staircase.

Ballard, who had been mate and later owner of the steamboat *Zephyr* running between Seattle and Olympia, was married in 1882. The couple lived in several rented homes before acquiring this property. Meanwhile Ballard had risen in the business world; he was one of the organizers of the Seattle National Bank in 1889 and after leaving it founded the Seattle Savings Bank. He was identified with several out-of-town banks as well and was a partner in the West Coast Land Co., which owned 700

acres on Salmon Bay. This was promoted as the district of Ballard, where land values rose spectacularly.

Ballard was inclined to move around. He went to New York and on his return took an apartment. He died in 1929.

This house on Minor Avenue eventually became the property of Swedish Hospital, which established a nurses home in it. In 1962 the dwelling became headquarters of the Pacific Northwest Research Foundation, where physicians could explore questions which arose in their daily practice. Ultra modern scientific equipment was installed in the former living room and the whole house became a laboratory for family doctors.

In West Seattle is a conspicuous log structure, reached by a little bridge over a tiny stream. It is Sea View Hall at 4004 Chilberg Avenue, erected about 1904 by John G. Maurer, an early day builder. He retrieved the vertical timbers from Puget Sound.

Maurer put up the three-story summer home shortly after his return from the Alaska gold rush. Formerly the building had its name across the front in letters made of pieces of driftwood.

The house has been converted into three apartments.

Known formerly for its monstrous bath tub and its "carriage lady," the Alfred H. Anderson house at 718 Minor Avenue, Seattle now is headquarters for Seattle University's Christian Activities Program. It has in the past served as McHugh Hall, men's living quarters, later as a women's dormitory. It has been owned by Seattle University since 1946.

Anderson, a timberman, built it in 1897. He organized the Mason County Logging Co. and was a partner in the formation of the Simpson Logging Co., besides being a large stockholder in several Seattle banks.

A man who weighed more than 300 pounds, he spared no expense to obtain a bath tub suited to his proportions. He ordered a custom-made tub seven feet eight inches long and 42 inches wide in New York. Part of the bath room wall had to be removed in order to install it. The manufacturer, taking no chances on breakage, made two identical tubs and presented the extra one to President William H. Taft.

Anderson's tub cost him $17,000 by the time the huge porcelain fixture was installed in a rather austere bath room, walled part way up with Alaska marble panels and floored with white mosaic tile.

Anderson died in 1914 and his widow lived on in the house until her death in 1940. She owned the last horse-drawn brougham in the city, using it until 1935. When she retired Lord and Lady, her aging team, she gave them and the carriage to William Guildenfeld, her silk-hatted coachman. Another of her carriages, the park hack, can be seen in the Museum of History and Industry, with Mrs. Anderson's initials in gold on the door. This was her light trap for country driving.

When her horse-and-carriage days terminated it was the end of an era for the neighborhood, where persons were accustomed to see Mrs. Anderson depart punctually at 10 o'clock every morning for her drive.

The Anderson carriage house is now a doctor's clinic.

A more permanent monument to the Anderson name is Anderson Hall, housing the College of Forestry at the University of Washington, given by the widow in honor of her husband. Mrs. Anderson, it might be added, was worth more than $12,000,000 at the time of her death.

This attractive Roman brick has graced the northeast corner of Spring Street and Boren Avenue since 1902 and has been the residence of the Catholic bishops of Seattle for 47 years. The mansion remains much as it was when built by W. D. Hofius, steel manufacturer. It is of late Italian Renaissance architecture, with liberal use of white terra cotta on the front and side where the porches have the effect of a loggia and the arches are elegantly carved. The roof is of copper with overhanging eaves. The fascia below the second-floor windows are unusual.

Inside the reception rooms are finished artistically in Honduras mahogany and there is a large fireplace faced with green Mexican onyx.

After the death of Mr. Hofius the family sold the house to Thomas M. Green in 1912 and that same year it was resold to Mr. and Mrs. Moses Prager, who occupied the residence until 1920 when the Corporation of the Catholic Bishop of Nisqually purchased it.

Bishop Edward John O'Dea lived there until his death in 1932 and Bishop Gerald Shaughnessy was the next occupant until he died in 1950. Since then Archbishop Thomas A. Connolly has made it his home.

The Albert S. Kerry mansion at 421 W. Highland Drive, Seattle, has been greatly modified since it was constructed in 1902. Then it had very small paned windows almost throughout and wide eaves. The latter have been shortened and boxed, the right side porch and the roof over the front terrace have been removed. Dormer windows are gone from the roof in front.

The remaining diamond panes are an example of the original decor.

Marvin E. Burke, the present owner, has transformed the mansion into a designer house. New work has been done both inside and out. The driveway and terraces have been changed, a pool installed and garden walls and steps relandscaped.

The house was notable when new for its four bed rooms with four baths, its seven fireplaces and its billiard room.

The Kerry family were the owners until late in the 1930's.

159

Among the few surviving great mansions on First Hill, Seattle is the Orion O. Denny home at 1204 Boren Avenue. Denny was the first white boy born in Seattle (July 17, 1853). He built in 1906 and after his death ten years later his widow leased the big stone-and-stucco house to George T. Myers, who purchased it in 1918.

Myers was a salmon packer, carrying on the industry in which his father had pioneered. The first Myers cannery was opened in Seattle in 1876 and the next year the son arrived in the city.

The Myers lived in the home 35 years and made numerous changes. The first year was spent remodeling. They removed leaded glass windows and sliding doors and installed a new staircase, arranging a suitable background for the many artistic furnishings they had purchased during their travels in Europe. To advise them in decorating they had Mrs. Edgar deWolfe, sister-in-law of Elsie deWolfe and mother of Winifred Hudnut (the former Mrs. Rudolph Valentino).

The Myers had excellent material to work with in the 14 rooms scattered on three floors. Some features were the gold and velvety blue tones of the library, the French drawing room with floor-to-ceiling mirrors, the garden room with black and white checkerboard floor, the master's bed room with marquetry floor, white marble fireplace and a blue canopied bed (Louis XVI), Mr. Myers' upstairs study with decorations from a Riviera chateau.

Mrs. Myers was a prominent club woman and was hostess for much entertaining, such as dinners and large benefit parties. Four weddings took place in the mansion.

Myers died in 1949 and the house was sold the following year to Dr. F. H. H. Kale.

Architects for the home were Bebb and Mendel. Before the era of large apartment buildings in the vicinity there was a splendid view from the windows. The place used to be surrounded by a rose hedge.

Offices of the Episcopal Church are in the former home of Mrs. Eliza Ferry Leary at 1551 Tenth Avenue E. Until 1935 it belonged to Washington's richest woman.

The house was erected in 1903-4 by John Leary at a cost of $50,000. He paid out more than double that sum for the land, terracing and exterior improvements. His total outlay has been estimated at $250,000.

Mr. Leary died early in 1905 before all of his plan was completed. He had intended that his and his partner's, P. P. Ferry's, mansions would occupy a 15-acre tract and have the advantages of scenery and seclusion, in other words be country places with the perquisites of town houses. The park would be laid out in the manner of English country estates; perhaps it would even have some deer.

The stables lay downhill from the house and the long winding driveway leading to them was to be the backbone of a scheme of landscape gardening. A low balustrade was to skirt the edge of the driveway where it passed along the brink of the bluff overlooking Lake Union.

Leary visualized the entire side of the hill as a

succession of terraces surmounted with beautiful homes.

He was a native of New Brunswick who had prospered in lumber and mercantile enterprises in the East. He visited Seattle in 1869 and decided to move there because railroads were expected soon to open the country. Leary was admitted to the bar and practiced law until 1882. He became mayor of Seattle two years later. He was active in promoting coal mines and railroads, he organized the gas company, owned a business building and was interested in the Puget Sound Navigation Co.

Mrs. Leary, daughter of the first state governor, was widely known as a club woman and social leader. She came to the Pacific Northwest in 1869 with her parents and married Leary in 1891. She was a charter member of the D.A.R. in Seattle.

The 14-room house was designed for entertaining, though some persons have described it as more like a church than a home. The architect was Alfred Bodley of England.

Paneled walls, stained glass windows and magnificent fireplaces were part of the decor. Belgian workers were brought in especially to prepare the paneling. On the main floor are a drawing room, sun room, hall, outer hall, gold room, dining room and library. The gold room is decorated in gold leaf. The kitchen was in an attached wing, described as being "in accord with modern ideas of keeping cooking odors away from living apartments."

Mrs. Leary was said to have had enough furnishings to fill two houses. Among the items was an Italian hand-carved dining room set made for Stanford White, a chair from a European palace and a Marie Antoinette sideboard.

Upon Mrs. Leary's death many of her possessions were auctioned to pay bequests in her will. So many of the curious were attracted to the sale that an admission of 15 cents was charged for the benefit of the Orthopedic Hospital.

The General Insurance Co. bought the home, expecting to convert it into executive offices and to erect a five-story office building on the property. The home would have been preserved as a show place. Instead, the firm gave it outright to the American Red Cross to provide quarters for wartime activities.

Eventually the Red Cross moved to a more central location and in 1948 the Episcopal Church raised money to purchase the home for its headquarters and for meeting rooms.

The Pierre P. Ferry home at 1229 Tenth Avenue E., which Leary had visualized as sharing the huge grounds. Ferry, brother of Mrs. Leary, died in 1932 and his widow lived on in the home another two years. It is now the dean's house for St. Mark's Cathedral.

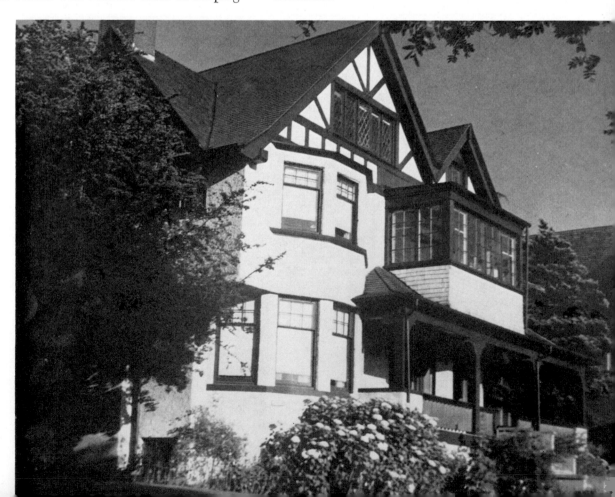

Haddon Hall, a famous manor in Derbyshire, England, was the model for the residence erected in 1902 by C. J. Smith, Seattle attorney, at 1147 Harvard Avenue E. Carl Nuese, of the firm of Cutter and Malmgren in Spokane, was the architect.

Now known as the bishop's house, it is occupied by the Rt. Rev. and Mrs. Ivol Ira Curtis. Since 1953 it has belonged to the Episcopal Diocese of Olympia.

The interior has outstanding woodwork and heraldic stained glass panels in the leaded windows. The carved plaster ceiling in the library was copied after that of Haddon Hall.

In 1936 Richard E. Lang purchased the house from a German count, who had occupied it for a time and had rebuilt much of the interior. The exterior has not been disturbed, except that the carriage house has become a three-car garage.

Lang made a gift of the house to the diocese.

Joshua Green's three-story brick, stucco and wood Tudor mansion was designed by Kirtland Cutter of Spokane and was built before 1906 by C. D. Stimson, Seattle lumberman. It is at 1204 Minor Avenue and is approached by a circular driveway and a carriage entrance.

The front door is of oak two inches thick and has a wrought iron knocker. The entrance hall is paneled with wood and there are beamed ceilings. In the house are six fireplaces, one guarded with carved wood lions and overhung with a massive carved bonnet. The dining room has sycamore panels. In addition to a built-in safe, there are some secret recesses concealed in other paneling.

Green, a banker who is approaching the century mark in age, has owned the house more than half of his lifetime. He said of this stately dwelling, "A man is measured by his home—not by its cost, but it should reflect his pride and his family."

Another Kirtland Cutter-designed home in Seattle is the Swiss chalet at Broadway and East Hamlin Street built in 1909 for Dr. Nils A. Johanson, founder and long-time head of Swedish Hospital. He was born in Lund, Sweden in 1872, came to the United States at 21 and moved to Seattle in 1907 to open a private practice. He was married the same year.

Almost immediately after moving to Washington the doctor urged founding of a new hospital. He fathered incorporation of Swedish Hospital in 1908. Dr. Johanson lived in his Swiss chalet until his death at 74 years.

The Cecil Callison home at 1901 10th Avenue E., Seattle, is an Eighteenth Century Italian villa erected in 1911 for Albert Rhodes of the Rhodes department store. The architect was Warren Gould.

The Callisons bought the property in 1958 along with many of the Rhodes' beautiful antiques. The house still has a formal garden, as when it was new. While the interior has been modernized considerably, the dining room contains some of the painted paneling put there by its original owner.

A variety of windows distinguishes the Harold K. Wilson home at the northwest corner of Harvard E. and Olive Way in Seattle, built in 1902 by George E. Bradley, office manager of the Stetson and Post sawmill. Additions were made to it in 1905 and 1929, but the best of the old features remain as they were.

The home has high beamed ceilings, plate rails, built-in seats, much paneling and carving. The first owner was desirous of showing what effects could be gained with the use of fir. Leaded and stained glass are in the windows and there is a tiled fireplace. The present garage started as a stable.

It is not difficult to distinguish Samuel Hill's taste for solid chateau types of masonry (see Maryhill) in this mansion he erected in 1909 at 814 E. Highland Drive, Seattle. Among the guests he entertained there were Marshal Joffre of France, Grand Duchess Marie of Russia and Queen Marie of Rumania and her children.

After Hill's death the house stood vacant a decade. Mr. and Mrs. Theodore Plestcheef purchased it in 1937, when like Maryhill, it was scarcely habitable. They spent two years rebuilding and searching for European-type furniture for it.

Now the house consists of two separate dwellings, Mrs. Plestcheef occupying the upper floors. The main floor apartment was the home of the late Mrs. Thomas D. Stimson.

The present Jeffrey B. Ewall house on East Madison Street near 38th Avenue E., Seattle was erected in 1908 by Samuel Hyde, who had lived in that city since 1888. The dwelling required two years to build. It has hand-painted, flower-garlanded ceilings, Tiffany light fixtures, onyx and tile fireplaces and leaded stained glass windows. The porch columns are topped with Corinthian capitals.

On the left of the central hall is the former music room; the present occupant does her weaving there on a loom.

The upstairs hall is as large as a living room and has a long upholstered seat on one side. At the head of the first landing on the stairs is a window made in Italy which reproduces the front door view through the columns, with Lake Washington and the distant mountains.

The master's bed room has a fireplace of Italian tile with swans. A mural runs around the dining room above the paneled wainscoting. A ball room is in the attic, a billiard room in the basement. Among other features are a wine cellar, a laundry with large drying room, clothes closets with stained glass windows, a huge tiled ice box (now electrified) and a back stairway with an electrically operated elevator seat. The former carriage house became a three-car garage.

The house is on half an acre of ground.

Among architects who early in the Twentieth Century brought about changes from the traditional in Seattle was Ellsworth Storey, who opened his office in 1903 and did original and creative work.

Here are some of his houses which broke away from current designs. The large white mansion at 3311 Cascadia Avenue S. was erected in 1907 and is owned by Mr. and Mrs. Arthur E. Lyon.

The house with an interesting cottage roof at 202 36th Avenue N. went up in 1909.

In 1908 Ellsworth Storey, designed these cottages to provide low rental homes in a good neighborhood. The brown wood siding has weathered pleasantly and blended with the setting. The integrity of design of these cottages has demonstrated the lasting qualities of good architecture. They are said never to remain vacant long.

Alexander Pantages, one of Seattle's most colorful figures in the entertainment world, built this home in 1909 at 36th Avenue and East Madison Street, adjoining Broadmoor. The residence cost approximately $50,000.

Pantages, a native of Greece, started his career in the Klondike. Before the gold rush dwindled he left in 1902 for Seattle with his profits and rented a theatre on Second Avenue. He established a circuit of theatres on the Pacific Coast. Although his last years were spent in California (he died there in 1936) he always considered Seattle and the Madison Avenue house his home.

Frank Brownell in 1910 commissioned this house at 1137 Harvard Avenue E., Seattle, from Carl F. Gould, architect. Two years later it was purchased by J. H. Bloedel, lumberman and financier, who occupied it until his recent death. His granddaughter, Mrs. T. H. Meadowcroft, is the present owner.

The residence is an adaptation of a French country house. It has a graceful stairway and contains two beautiful chandeliers—a French one of rock crystal and in the library a Tole chandelier.

An Elizabethan half-timbered house at 2812 Mount St. Helens Place S. built in 1911 for Joseph Kraus. It belongs to the day when 17-room homes were still desired in elite circles.

The Frank H. Osgood home, built in 1903 at 678 W. Prospect Street, Seattle, was designed by R. Clipston Sturgis & Barton, Boston architects. It was pictured in a 1919 issue of House Beautiful magazine and described as a New England colonial patterned after Hyslop House in Brookline, Mass. It was remodelled in 1927. David M. Checkley is the present occupant.

Frank H. Osgood moved to Seattle in 1884 and organized the first horse car lines and built the Yesler Way cable car route. He retired to Santa Barbara in 1926 and died in 1934. Mrs. Osgood was a garden lover and an authority on good architecture and furniture.

Early pictures show the residence in large grounds and standing at the top of a slope facing a sweeping view of Mount Rainier and Elliott Bay. At the rear was a formal garden. The property once included the entire city block, but when Paul Harper purchased it, he sold lots on the north and built a brick wall around the remaining land.

Harper was an active civic leader and hosted New Year's tea dances and many other memorable social events in the big house.

The rooms are spacious as might be supposed. There are five bed chambers and four baths on the second floor, three bed rooms and two baths on the third. A wing to the right contains servants rooms on the second floor over a large pantry and laundry.

Drawing room, library and dining room all have fireplaces and there are three more in the bed rooms. Other rooms are a sun room, huge entrance hall, ball room and billiard room.

Each year recently the Washington State District chapter, American Institute of Interior Designers, has cooperated with Seattle philanthropies in creating a designer show house for public inspection. The 1968 choice was a pink stucco Mediterranean-style villa at 1254 Tenth Avenue E., opposite St. Mark's Episcopal Cathedral.

The mansion, designed by Walter Oates, was

built in 1910 by Wallace Collins, a railroad and lumber executive. It was sold in 1921 to Elijah Sherman Grammer, member of a logging firm, who was appointed to fill out an unexpired term as United States senator in 1932.

Some alterations were made in the house after the Grammers moved in. The Philippine koa wood stairway and foyer paneling were replaced with a marble staircase and bronze balustrade. Hand-painted designs were added to the ceiling beams.

Other features in the house are a small paneled library, huge living and dining rooms, much marble and tile, conservatories off each side of the main floor, a garden with gazebo and fountain, basement ball room and wine vault and a third floor arranged like a separate apartment for servants.

As originally built the roof line was quite different, with a tile-topped tower on one corner and many third-floor windows. These have been removed as well as some of the arched porches which surrounded the lower story.

After Grammer's death his widow and her niece stayed on until the house was sold to William Gross.

Presidents of the University of Washington have their official residence in Hillcrest, the mansion at 808 36th Avenue E., Seattle, built in 1906 by Mr. and Mrs. Edwin Gardner Ames and her parents, Mr. and Mrs. William Walker. It belonged both in the Ames and Walker estates. The Ames went on living there after the Walkers died. The Ames had no children, so made the University their beneficiary and offered the house as a residence for the president. The first to live there was President E. Lyle Spencer in 1932.

As the original owners were engaged in the lumber industry, they used the best quality of fir in the construction and had matched panels of it in the entrance hall. The library (formerly the music room) is in Honduras mahogany. Some of the paneling is now painted white.

Bebb and Mendel were architects for the house. In 1928 the Ames added a sun room, now the second-floor living room of the president's family, and installed an organ on the landing. The house was again renovated in 1959, one wall of the dining room was knocked out to open it to a glassed-in terrace room overlooking the rose garden. This has

shojis on the outside to screen it from the street. The kitchen was remodeled for serving large numbers of persons. Between 300 and 400 guests can be accommodated at a stand-up party.

Some of the furniture has been in the dwelling since it was built, including an Italian dining set, cut glass and silver.

Dr. Charles E. Odegaard's is the fifth presidential family to occupy the house. Any changes in it are supervised by the University's School of Architecture and some of the decorating by the Art Department. The second floor has a complete apartment for the president, the first floor being largely for official use.

This elegant Seattle estate on Lake Washington has had several prominent owners, among them H. F. Ostrander, Louis Dulien and George Gunn. Least well known today was its builder, Jules (Julius) Redelsheimer, who had a peculiar claim to fame at the beginning of the present century. He owned a clothing store at First Avenue and Columbia Street

that had a mosaic in the sidewalk in front, studded with silver dollars.

Among Redelsheimer's early publicity stunts were mule racing, pie-eating contests and throwing bundles of merchandise from the roof of his store. He had the first escalator in Seattle. He was one of the best known citizens, was prominent in kennel clubs and had many private charities. Dog breeding was his hobby.

Although Redelsheimer had no children, he wanted a huge house, terraced grounds and a boat dock. He looked forward to the time when there would be a canal and he could take a yacht from his new home to his store.

Accordingly he bought property in Denny Blaine Park when it was a long way out and determined to make his estate a show place. The house, begun in 1910, had eight bed rooms and four baths. It faced 141 feet of lakeshore, equipped with a boat house, cabana and tennis court. Across the street behind the house was a four-car garage with apartment.

"I don't know why I built so big a house," Redelsheimer said when he was about ready to move in. "There's only me and mother. But I'm going to

make it as complete as possible. After it's finished I'm going to round up all of my friends and it is going to be as much theirs as it is mine."

He never was able to carry out his intention, for the housewarming never came off.

One day, when the house was almost ready for occupancy and its furnishings were ordered, Redelsheimer was taking stock in his store (which had lately celebrated its twenty-fourth anniversary) when he was felled by a stroke. He died suddenly in 1914 at the age of 61 and no Redelsheimer ever lived in the 26-room house, then acclaimed as among the most beautiful in the city.

King County

One of the few reminders of the time when Peter Kirk, English steel mill builder, intended to make Kirkland, Washington, a manufacturing center, is the brick house at 526 10th Avenue W. Three brick buildings still stand on Market Street as monuments to Kirkland's aspirations to become a steel center, but residences of that day are harder to find.

Kirk built a turreted, many-gabled home for himself near the 200 block on Waverly Way and erected four brick houses for key personnel of the mill slightly north of his own home. The one built for John George Kellett, chief engineer, survives and is now occupied by the George Harris family. The Kirk house, a frame structure, disappeared in 1911.

When the depression of 1893 put an end to the steel mill just as it was ready for operation, Kellett moved away and his dwelling was occupied for 20 years or more by a widow who rented rooms.

The house formerly had porches all around it. The bay windows and arched window frames upstairs and the brickwork itself stem from English ideas as to how a mill-town residence should look.

More than a million dollars was lost in Kirkland in its year of hard times. The Great Western Iron & Steel Co. was to have manufactured railroad rails from iron ore brought from the Cascade Mountains. A brick plant near the boat landing was one of the industries which opened during the boom period.

There are doors on every side of the rambling activities center at Marymoor County Park, near Lake Sammamish. This is a rear entrance to what was the farm house, or country estate, of James W. Clise, Seattle financier. When he owned the place it was called Willow Moor.

About 1904 Clise acquired 80 willow-fringed acres on the Sammamish River, erected a hunting lodge and established a water-fowl preserve. Three years later he made extensive additions to the five-room cottage and added a second story. Meanwhile he more than tripled his acreage and commenced breeding Ayreshire cows and Morgan horses. His gardens were elaborate, being not only utilitarian but containing many ornamental plants.

By 1907 the Clises had moved from the city to their 28-room country retreat. It had two huge fireplaces, beamed ceilings, a ball room and an orchid conservatory. It became the scene of parties and dances. Among the guests who visited it was a high-ranking Japanese nobleman, Baron Shibuwasa, who brought 40 attendants with him and spent a day there in 1913 photographing the grounds and studying methods on the model farm. He selected Clise's home as an example of the American way of life.

The house now is a multi-purpose park facility, containing a historical museum, several spacious meeting rooms and district headquarters for the sheriff's staff in that part of King County.

In rehabilitating the Clise estate the County Park Department reactivated a windmill on the grounds. Clise had some Dutch ancestors and on a visit to The Netherlands he saw a certain windmill which he decided to copy. It was equipped to pump water and grind grain.

In those days water in the Sammamish River was higher than at present (it was lowered by construction of the Lake Washington Ship Canal). One could go easily by boat to Clise's landing and he located his mill close by, liking to see its turning arms as he arrived home from the city.

Today's Redmond Golf Club was once the home of the man for whom the town is named, Luke McRedmond. It was likewise for a time Redmond's first hotel.

Luke McRedmond came from Ireland in 1869, lived two years in Kitsap County, then rowed up the Duwamish and Black Rivers and through Lake Washington to Lake Sammamish to settle on a homestead. He took his possessions along with him on a scow.

McRedmond homesteaded where the golf club now is and built his big home there around the turn of the century.

Aaron S. Neely, born in Tennessee in 1849, crossed the plains as a boy of seven with his parents, Mr. and Mrs. David A. Neely, who took a donation claim below Kent and were the first settlers in the immediate neighborhood. They were compelled soon to move closer to Seattle because of Indian hostilities.

Neely's father enlisted to fight the Indians after the White River massacre while the family remained in the little fort on the Henry Van Asselt farm in the Duwamish Valley. After three years they returned to their own place.

Aaron, eldest of seven children, went to school near the farm and put in one year at the Territorial University. Then he managed his father's property. The young man married at 27 and preempted a 120-acre claim a mile west of Auburn. He cut a road through a veritable jungle to the place and lived there two years. He next filed on 120 acres of railroad land at what is now East Auburn. To this he added other pieces, gradually clearing the heavy timber and bringing the tract under production. He set out 400 apple trees.

Here he built a pretentious home, cutting the lumber for it at his own sawmill on the property. The gingerbread trim was turned on a hand lathe.

By this time he needed many rooms, for he had six children. Upstairs he provided four bed rooms and on the ground floor a parlor, sitting room, dining room and kitchen. Being in the country he still had to light with candles and lamps. Those in the

main room were fixtures that hung from medallions and pulled down from the ceiling.

Neely lived in this house until 1900, becoming one of the leading fruit growers and farmers of the area. He then leased the farm to his son, bought property in Auburn and erected another house for his retirement years.

The big house is now unused except for a portion occupied by a Filipino farmer. Although the dwelling stood on low ground, it was never invaded by floods until 1960, when an embankment built for a new freeway created a dam and trapped the water, which stood 18 inches deep on the floors the Neelys had so proudly kept polished.

Olalla

Buena Vista, Good View, was the name Charles Nelson gave the turreted mansion he built on a slope south of Olalla, overlooking Colvos Passage and Vashon Island. He had arrived in Olalla in 1889, took a homestead, worked on Puget Sound steamboats and prospered in the logging and mill days. In 1904 he returned from a stay in Alaska during the gold rush and bought the store in the tiny harbor and became postmaster. For a long time the family lived behind the store and rented rooms above, Mrs. Nelson providing meals. In 1914 they moved into the new house, built entirely of Pacific Northwest products.

Nelson had the first telephone in the area and the first Model T. He was notary public and in wartime served on the ration board and sold war bonds.

The couple resided in the big house the remainder of their lives. After Mrs. Nelson died it stood idle for a time, then their son, Carl V. Nelson, moved in and modernized the place, preserving as much of its old flavor as possible.

The elder Mrs. Nelson never threw anything away; her old wash machine and wood stove were in the basement and much of the Victorian furniture remained. The attic was filled with documentary treasure—letters, mail-order catalogues, clippings, photographs, telephone books and files of newspapers no longer in existence.

With automobile roads Olalla has lost its isolation, but nothing has crowded in on the house on the hill; it is the most striking object on the landscape as one approaches by boat.

Pierce County and Tacoma

This ranch dwelling at Eatonville was erected in 1904 by Alfred Conrad, a German immigrant. He needed a roomy home, for he had half a dozen or more children.

In 1922 a fire swept through the area, setting the roof ablaze, but Conrad fortunately had installed a trap door and was able to carry water and extinguish his burning shingles. Thus he saved the rest of the house. When he made repairs he resorted to corrugated iron roofing in order to avert any repetition.

Conrad operated his farm and was employed as an assessor, timber cruiser and surveyor. Although he died in 1950 at the age of 87, his home is still in the family, occupied by one of his married daughters.

The Ezra Meeker house on Pioneer Avenue in Puyallup, more recently the Valley Nursing Home, was scheduled to be converted into a museum and moved to another property. The metal trim on the roof, cornices, gables, round-topped windows and covered carriage entrance distinguish it.

Inside are decorative wood facings on the fireplaces and an impressive entrance hall and staircase. Beneath the stairs is a guest closet with built-in umbrella rack and drawers for overshoes.

Ezra Meeker was Puyallup's most celebrated citizen, whose statue stands in the central square. He died in 1928 shortly before his 98th birthday. He came to Washington by prairie schooner in 1852, prospered as a hop-grower and farmer and became well known for his writings on agricultural subjects and his books on pioneers.

The view is from one side and does not show all of the gingerbread trim on the house nor its six chimneys. It is believed to have been built about 1890.

After Meeker's death great quantities of his papers were found in the attic. They are now in the State Historical Society library at Tacoma.

Sumner's public library is in itself a period piece, for the oldest part was constructed in 1875 for George Ryan and his bride, Lucy V. Wood, who traveled from Baraboo, Wis. to marry him. Ryan, employed as bookkeeper at the Port Gamble mill, met her in San Francisco and they were married there. They went to Tacoma by steamship and to Puyallup by rowboat, thence up the valley by wagon.

The cabin had been built by two friends named Avery and Hall while Ryan earned the price of the materials by staying on his job at the mill.

Ryan established a sawmill of his own two miles northeast of Sumner. It was reached by a plank road, very noisy to drive. He brought logs downhill on a greased chute to his pond.

Soon after the town had been named Mrs. Ryan woke up one morning to find letter boxes and mail bags dumped at her front door. She carried on as postmaster for a while, with the help of a man to bring the mail from Puyallup.

Ryan prospered and in 1891 became the town's first mayor. He built a large hall for a skating rink, had a farm and hop kiln. His sons ran a store.

The main part of the house dates from the 1880's. It has a spindle-trimmed porch and the windows upstairs are bordered with colored panes. The fireplace was made of bricks hauled from Steilacoom in 1875. The old section of the house was restored in 1930, using furnishings of the earlier period. A few historic objects are displayed in the library, among them a yoke from Ryan's logging oxen and a sample of wooden water pipe made at his mill.

Shelton

Although now an office building of the Simpson Timber Co in Shelton, this colonial house was built in 1920 by Mr. and Mrs. Mark E. Reed for their own home. The architect was Joseph Wohleb of Olympia.

The Reeds moved an earlier residence to make room for the new house. One portion of the original was placed across the street as quarters for Mrs. Reed's mother, Mrs. Sol Simpson, widow of the company founder. Another part is a block away and became the Christian Science Church.

Highest quality domestic lumber and veneers were employed throughout the new house. None of it was of local origin because the Simpson company did not have a sawmill in Shelton until 1925.

On the lower floor on either side of the entrance always were two offices. Reed served seven terms in the Washington House of Representatives and for a time was speaker. His office in one end of the colonial house was often termed "the little statehouse" because so many persons visited him on political matters. Mrs. Reed had the office in the opposite end, where she carried on philanthropic work and her duties as a Shelton school board director. During this period Reed gave the community a new high school building, which was named for his wife.

The Reeds moved from Shelton to Seattle in 1930, three years preceding Mr. Reed's death. His wife survived him by several years.

After the couple departed the residence was altered and made into a guest house for both Simpson's and Rayonier's Shelton operations. This continued until the early 1960's, when the home was converted into additional office space.

The building is maintained very much as it appeared when the Reeds resided there. At the landing of the first flight of graceful stairs still stands the small organ played many years ago by Mrs. Sol Simpson. The house was the scene of weddings, receptions, management meetings, retirement parties, pinochle gatherings and the Mark E. Reed Scholarship Foundation dinners for many years after it ceased to be a family home.

For 12 years no one had lived at 513 North E Street in Tacoma and the place, near the Tacoma Tennis Club, had been considered an eyesore until the American Plywood Association purchased it in 1967. Using it as a challenge to show how wood could transform a derelict, the association refurbished the home without robbing it of its Victorian charm.

New roofing was laid and fancy butt shingles were added on the exterior. Some siding was replaced with plywood panels. Inside a few ceilings were lowered, the butler's pantry was removed, also some other walls.

Once the changes were completed the association had no trouble finding an occupant for this quaintly charming residence.

This house at 4305 North Forty-second Street, Tacoma was erected about 1893 by a development company and was purchased five or six years later by the Rev. Calvin W. Stewart, who was president of Whitworth College, then at Sumner. For the next five years it was occupied by the Rev. Amos Fox, who taught mathematics and preceded Stewart briefly as president of the school.

Whitworth was moved to Tacoma in January, 1900 and remained there nearly 15 years. By this time Stewart already had retired as its head to become financial secretary of the college, remaining in this post until 1902

In 1904 the Stewart family moved into the residence and continued to occupy it the next 40 years. Afterward it changed hands a couple of times, one of the occupants operating a shop, "The House of Antiques," on the premises. The present owner of the home is Lester R. Finkas.

Oak was the wood used for much of the interior finishing, combined with leaded glass. On the staircase are two stained glass windows. Ceilings are ten feet high. There are three fireplaces on the main floor and one in the master's bed room. The house was lighted by gas around the turn of the century and a hand-cranked machine for producing it is a fixture in the basement.

Divided into apartments, the old George Lewis Gower colonial home at 417 North E Street, Tacoma (upper right) does not look much as it did in 1906 when Russell and Babcock featured it in a booklet covering the firm's recent architectural designs.

The shingles were then stained a dark color and the three porticoes were connected by a porch with a low railing. There was a covered sleeping porch over the left-hand entrance and a wooden railing on both it and the upstairs porch at the opposite side. A storm door enclosed the main entrance, creating a vestibule.

Gower, the first owner, was president of the Foster Lumber Co. and the Gower-Foster Co., timberland dealers. For many years afterward the place was the home of the Howarth family.

Another picture in the Russell and Babcock booklet was of the house that firm designed in 1898 for Richard Vaeth, Tacoma jeweler and optician. It stands at 422 North E Street, but is shorn of some of its earlier splendor in the form of an elaborate frieze of festoons entirely around the house above the second story. The framed spaces above the third floor windows likewise once were filled with ornamental motifs.

The shape of the porch roof and the chimney

with two windows are distinctive.

A. J. Russell and Everett P. Babcock planned many of Tacoma's large homes of the period just before and after the turn of the century. Russell was born in India and studied in Europe, particularly in the Paris Beaux Arts. He was employed by Boston, Kansas City and St. Louis architects before coming west. Babcock was from New York and his first work on the Coast was when he supervised construction of Tacoma's Carnegie Library.

Though not as old as other dwellings in this book, the John Philip Weyerhaeuser mansion at 4301 N. Stevens Street, Tacoma deserves attention as a landmark, for it represents the peak of the big-house period, the turning point as it were. The mansion went through a period when no one wanted to live in it because it was too ostentatious. Like other huge homes of the era of affluence, when keeping several servants presented no problem, this one has seen other uses. It has been a residence for student nuns and only lately has been converted into housing for honor students at the University of Puget Sound.

When Weyerhaeuser died in 1935 at the age of 76 he was one of the nation's best known lumbermen and had actively directed his firm almost until the time of his death. He was born in Illinois, worked in his father's lumber mills during school vacations and soon after graduation became manager of the Rock Island Lumber and Manufacturing Co. From this he went on to managing other mills and expanding them. He was elected a director of the Weyerhaeuser companies in 1914 and then president. He and his wife moved to Tacoma in 1916.

Shortly after the end of the First World War he erected Haddaway Hall, the name he gave his home. It was a great showplace and scene of many affairs, as Mrs. and Mrs. Weyerhaeuser were active in civic, church and philanthropic circles.

It was designed in the style of an English manor by F. B. Meade and James Hamilton, Cleveland ar-

chitects. Construction was of brick and it was protected on all approaches by a brick wall. A noted Boston landscape architect named Olmstead designed the grounds, which had been part of the campus of Whitworth College. Several ornamental columns from the old president's house were saved and used to good effect in the garden.

The Weyerhaeuser home was completed in 1923. It has 16 principal rooms, many of them with sweeping views. Tall leaded-glass windows give a cathedral effect to the main hall, where there is a pipe organ.

Mrs. Weyerhaeuser died in 1933 and when her husband followed three years later the mansion was put up for sale, as none of the heirs wished such pretentious quarters.

George G. Franklin, head of the Franklin Food Stores, purchased the house and changed the name to Seamont. Although it is reported that $500,000 was invested in the home and its sweeping five and a half acres of gardens, he purchased it for $26,000 and the back taxes. Values were extremely low as the result of the depression.

Franklin did not live long in the house, for it became a place of terror for him and his wife. He received threats of kidnapping his child, which went so far as to the finding of a ladder propped against the wall below a bedroom window. Young Charles Mattson had been kidnapped from the house next door and never was seen alive again. The Franklins wanted no such experience, so they moved out.

Orcas Island

Robert Moran, head of Moran Brothers shipyard and former mayor of Seattle, fell in love with the San Juan Islands when he went past them to Roche Harbor in 1898 on his way to Alaska with a fleet of Yukon River steamers built by his company. In 1904 he was back again looking over the islands and gathering literature about them. Before long it be-

came known that he was buying parcels of land in the names of other members of the family. By July, 1905 Moran Brothers owned 2,400 acres on Orcas Island and in another six months it was announced they were retiring to their new property, having sold their business to eastern capitalists. Eventually the Morans controlled about 7,000 acres.

On the shore at what had been Newhall (so named for a mill operator who turned out lumber, box shooks and lime-barrel staves) Robert Moran founded a baronial estate, its center a mansion he

built to stand for centuries. Since he was a ship-builder, his island home had certain resemblances to a battleship. His fruit room had a metal ship's door and the laundry was equipped with a battery of cement tubs with fixed copper washboards. The drying room was fitted with movable racks and electric heat like a ship's laundry.

The family safe in the basement was enclosed in a vault. To extract valuables from it one had to open five doors. A key cabinet in the entrance hall contained nearly 500 keys, numbered and tagged. Doors throughout the house had massive hinges, each with a lignum vitae bearing. On the balcony surrounding the great music room were two libraries, each centered with a ship-carpentered desk with small drawers for storing photographs.

Other work with an air of permanence went into creating the room with billiard and pool tables on the lower floor and two bowling alleys.

Before Moran erected the house he built a machine shop at Newhall, the name of which he changed to Rosario, and moved equipment from his Seattle shipyard. He employed between 50 and 60 men on the island, working in wood, steel and bronze. Some were responsible for the mahogany paneling, copper roof, teak marquetry floors and certain heavy furnishings. These men also built a large pleasure yacht in the workshop.

The music room in the great mansion was arranged for staging private theatricals and stereopticon lectures. An organ and a grand piano were part of the equipment. It is said Moran played the organ himself and often wakened guests with it. He insisted they observe his Spartan rising and retiring hours.

Large parties were accomodated at the house and Moran made known he could sleep 200 guests if necessary.

The builder passed 27 years of his life on Orcas and is reputed to have spent more money in the islands than any other citizen of the San Juans. He wearied of the mansion after his wife's death in 1932 and six years later sold it to a California steel manufacturer, Donald L. Rheem. The latter lavished hundreds of thousands of dollars on improvements, filling the house with works of art, oriental rugs, crystal, silver and linens, installing a projection room for motion pictures, equipping a dispensary and small exercise room with health appliances.

The Rheems left in 1958 and the place changed hands several times. It is now a hotel, tastes in baronial estates having changed, influenced by the costs of upkeep and high taxes.

Central Washington (Yakima and Douglas Counties)

David Longmire went to the Wenas, in Yakima County, to make his home in 1869, choosing land that had belonged to Chief Owhi and his people. When Longmire had passed through with his father's wagon train in 1853 and camped near this spot the travelers bought potatoes and green vegetables grown on the Indian gardens and these sustained them on the trip over Naches Pass.

Dave was nine years old at that time, but he remembered the gardens and wanted to return to them. He lived in a log cabin until 1884, then built this home. It formerly had verandas on both sides and much gingerbread and was considered the showplace of the valley.

The Longmires raised their seven children here. The couple lived in the house the remainder of their lives, Longmire dying in 1925 and his widow in 1949. Mrs. Roy Longmire, a daughter-in-law, still lives there. The house has been continuously in the one family.

The Frank Kandle home at Wenas, Yakima County, was the post office at that place from 1899 to 1939. Kandle went to the Upper Wenas in the late 1870's, then returned to Olympia (where he had been since 1852) and married Ida R. Green. Their first home was a log cabin, where the three children were born. The cabin burned in 1891 and this house was built. It was T-shaped with porches. This is a rear view, as construction was in progress on the front side when the photographer visited the place.

Kandle raised livestock and a dairy herd and did general farming. His wife was postmistress for seven years.

In 1906 Kandle sold his home and moved away because of a shortage of water on Wenas Creek. Earl B. Evans bought the place and continued the office of postmaster. Col. Grant S. Green is the present owner.

Jasper Nelson built the house below in 1905 or thereabout to replace a previous dwelling which had stood at Lower Naches, Yakima County and served as an inn. The older log home, belonging to his father, John Nelson, had burned.

The elder Nelsons crossed the plains in 1846 and, after living in Oregon, moved to the Naches in 1864 and became the first white settlers in the valley. Father and son operated a ferry at Painted Rocks, using a team to pull wagons across the river on a barge. Later they built a bridge of cottonwood logs.

A stage route was inaugurated from The Dalles to Ellensburg and Jasper drove a coach until arrival of the Northern Pacific Railroad in 1885 put an end to that business.

Jasper Nelson's home is owned now by R. D. Scofield. The Sun Tides Golf Course occupies a large portion of the former Nelson property, where once the family raised fruit and hops.

Robert Scott, Sr. built this house at Naches in 1889 and his family lived in it until 1900, when it was sold to the Tennant and Miles Land Co.

Scott and his sons were contractors and painters. They arrived in North Yakima in 1884 and the following year built the Yakima Hotel.

Much of the lumber for their own house was hauled from The Dalles. A large home was needed, as there were six boys and a daughter. The family established the first irrigation ditch in the South Naches area, taking water out of the Naches River. They raised all kinds of field crops until 1891, when the place was planted to hops. Their large hop house is still standing.

After the land company purchased the property it was divided into 40-acre tracts and orchards were set out. One of the purchasers, William Kauzlarich, acquired the picturesque house and lived in it the rest of his life. A young member of the Kauzlarich family owns the place.

The Yakima Women's Club house at 302 Second Street, built in 1908, was the former home of George Donald, banker, rancher, railroad and ditch builder. He arrived in Yakima in 1884 with the Northern Pacific and constructed branch lines to Naches, Cowiche, Zillah, Moxee and White Swan. He was responsible for construction of the first large irrigation canal, the Kiona (later part of the Sunnyside Canal). In 1888, when the Yakima National Bank was organized, he became its president.

Donald lived in this house all the latter part of his life. When his widow's estate was settled in 1929 the Twentieth Century Club and the Women's Club merged and became the Women's Century Club. It bought the house and did much modernizing. The dining room remains as it was in the Donalds' time.

The Horace M. Gilbert House at 2109 W. Yakima Avenue, Yakima, built in 1898, has been filled with antiques by the present occupants, William Donelson and his artist wife.

A turret room, walled with diamond-shaped shingles, is part of an upstairs sun porch. The shingles continue around the upper story and match diamond panes in the upper halves of downstairs windows.

The library has an art glass window in shades of brown and yellow. These colored panes correspond with others lighting the central staircase.

Gilbert came west in 1897 from Illinois, where he had farmed extensively. He purchased 20 acres a mile west of Yakima, improved the tract and erected his home there. In 1899, with two partners, he organized the Richey and Gilbert Co., one of the oldest produce firms dealing in hay, grain and fruits. The company leased and cleared 2,000 acres near Toppenish and shipped carloads of livestock and produce. Gilbert became president of the Central Bank of Toppenish.

It was taken for granted that any small-town banker would have a large home, so back about 1912 Al Rogers built this one in Waterville. Rogers was considerably more than a banker in the Douglas County community; he ran a general store and developed the Waterville Railway Co., running between that town and Douglas.

The third floor of the home contained a well equipped gymnasium. Judging from the rows of windows, Rogers must have been a believer in plenty of fresh air. Probably his health was much on his mind.

Dr. John E. Gahringer, Jr., present occupant, found many souvenirs of Rogers in the house, although the family had been gone for years. The original owner was a good friend of Sam Hill, whose autographed picture, escorting Queen Marie of Rumania, turned up among the scattered souvenirs.

Okanogan and Ferry Counties

Like something from another world, this stone house, picturesque and alone, stands at the top of the Mineral Hill grade a mile west of Conconully, Okanogan County. It was built late in the last century for Charles Herrman, pioneer merchant and farmer. He homesteaded around 1898 and was one of the first storekeepers in the town. He left this business to raise cattle on the ranch where he lived until 1940.

The house was strictly a local product, down to the very lime in the mortar, burned in kilns not far from Conconully. Remnants of the ovens still may be seen.

Ed Stickle, a rock mason, was the builder. The lumber he used was from a local saw mill. The house had three rooms with a combination barn and lean-to storage space attached. A rock fireplace was in the living room.

Herrman, born in Germany, came directly to Conconully from the old country. He married Mrs. Virginia Grainger, a widow who was the first super- intendent of schools in Okanogan County.

Though Herrman lived some distance from town, he never owned a car. He always rode horseback or walked.

The Mason Thurlow ranch home at Beaver Creek in the Methow Valley is five miles below Twisp. Near it is the first small cabin made of driftwood logs caught in the streams at high water by Joe White, who took out a squatter's right to the place in 1886. His cabin had a sod roof and an earth floor.

Thurlow bought a homestead relinquishment of White the following year, giving $22.50 for the cabin and 160 acres. The initial voting in the Methow Valley was done in this cabin in the fall of 1888 during the Hays-Tilden campaign. Twelve votes were cast, nine of them for the Republican candidate for President. Thurlow entertained the voters with a dinner of venison stew.

Needing larger quarters before he could bring in his family, Thurlow built a second home in 1888, a two-room log dwelling shown as the back part of the house in the picture. The dwelling was enlarged as the family grew. It was basically entirely of logs, but was later covered with boards and painted white. The first plaster Thurlow used he made him- self of lime, sand and cow hair.

When he went out over the mountains to bring in his wife and four children Mrs. Thurlow died in Ellensburg. Mr. and Mrs. Isaac Nickell came in with the party and soon after their arrival Nickell died. Mrs. Nickell cared for her own two children and the motherless Thurlows. She married the latters' father in 1892 and they had seven more children, so needed a big house for so many offspring.

The last Thurlow son, Frank, and his wife keep the home refurbished as a memorial to their parents. It has been redecorated inside, but contains some of the antique furniture which always belonged there.

This was built by William Magee at Twisp about 1902. Only four families have owned it. Eldie Magee and family lived there until 1921 when Allen Wetzel, lumber mill operator bought it. He sold in the 1930's to Dr. John W. Malzacher, who used the upstairs for his office and had rooms for patients who needed care for minor surgery or maternity cases. His wife, a nurse, helped him.

The residence was last occupied by the Perry Novotneys.

The George H. Wiltz house in Chesaw is unusual, in that it is made of hand-axed planks set upright. It was built in 1902 by Nelson Holmes in the hills above town and was hauled to Chesaw about five years ago.

The massive upright corner timbers had been mounted on a foundation and then the solid walls were added and strengthened with others mortised diagonally, each plank shaped with hand saw and wood chisel to fit perfectly into grooves gouged in the wall timbers. The timbers supporting the gables are also hand hewn, the rafters being smaller than the uprights in the first story.

The original owner moved away before completing the structure and it was not much lived in. The Wiltzes, after moving it, recaulked the walls with putty, removed the hand-made shakes and shingled the roof, stained the walls and furnished their retirement home with period pieces to match the setting.

The Wheaton family moved on this property at Toroda Creek about 1908 and built a house of squared logs to replace the small log cabin, still standing. After Mrs. Wheaton's death the place was sold to Dr. Schrock, who turned it into a cattle ranch. It has changed hands several times since but continues to be a cattle ranch.

The house has one recent addition, a new corrugated metal roof.

Believe it or not, this railroad station is Fairfield's oldest residence. Erected in 1888, it accompanied a large wooden water tank for the then Washington and Idaho Railroad, later the O.W.R. & N. and after that part of the Union Pacific.

Because Fairfield had a large spring adjacent to the right of way the site for the station was selected and a settlement grew around it. As there were no other habitations at first, the railroad provided quarters for its stationmaster. He was enabled to

Lincoln County

observe the track signals without leaving his rooms.

Fairfield was the last of the towns to spring up along the line. The rails bypassed older Hangman's Creek (Alpha), which already had a post office. The latter community gave up and died.

An interesting brick, built before 1904 by Martines Olson, banker and merchant of Reardon, Lincoln County. He moved away long ago and only his house remains as a monument to him. Note the ornamentation of the gables and the neat brickwork around the living room windows.

Pride in workmanship is demonstrated in the decoration of this modest residence on a tree-lined and quiet street in Davenport. In its heyday the place was a jewel-like example of one man's castle.

There must have been special names for these decorative forms in the old millwork catalogues, but now who would order jigsawed brackets, finials, rosettes and band-sawed cresting and what carpenter would know where to put them?

The house was built by Joseph A. Hoople, born in 1835 in a community 80 miles west of Montreal, Canada. He moved to the United States in his sixteenth year, graduated from Oberlin College and took out citizenship papers. In 1886 he settled in Davenport, opened a harness shop, did a thriving business and held stock in several valuable mines. For 14 years he was Davenport's city treasurer. His son, Archie, now occupies the family home.

Malcolm McInnis, who with two partners had the largest lumber business in the Big Bend country, built the house opposite in 1899 at 1001 Morgan Street, Davenport. It was extremely well constructed, as McInnis was also a contractor and in a position to employ the best of materials.

In 1907 the place was sold to Jack B. Adams, who lived there the rest of his life. He was from Kentucky, moving to Washington in 1885 and operating a farm in the Rocklyn district. He kept several race horses on his ranch. Adams divided his time between the country property and his residence in Davenport. Upon his death he left a large estate. As his son did not survive the parents, the property was divided between 19 cousins.

Lew Hutsell purchased the house in 1954, remodeled it considerably and now Mrs. Hutsell has an antique shop in it.

Spokane

When Spokane wasn't much more than a village it boasted millionaire homes, accounted for by the quartz mining rush to the nearby Coeur d'Alenes. Compared to other parts of the nation Spokane's season of depression around the 1893 panic was short lived. The city was for the time being the mining capital of the United States and thronged with fortune hunters, capitalists and investors. Nowhere else were the gay nineties gayer.

One of the men who arrived early in Spokane was James Nettleton Glover, coming from Salem, Ore. in May, 1873. He paid $4,000 for a squatter's right, built a store and traded with the Indians. From the time of his arrival Spokane began to grow.

Among the oldest houses in the city is Glover's. Formerly it stood where the Paulsen Building is. It

survived the fire of August, 1889 and was purchased that year by S. P. M. Richards.

Glover gloated that he had sold to a sucker from Kansas for $10,000. He didn't want to see the house torn down and it never has been. Moved to West 725 First Avenue, it was rebuilt and much changed and is now rented out as apartments. When Ralph H. Griffith bought it in 1959 he razed the old servants' quarters, stable and hay shed. The house itself still contains some hand-wrought nails. Somebody has described its architecture as "modified Missourian."

Glover traveled to Spokane on horseback and cooked his first meals over a campfire beside the falls. Sixteen years later he was a banker and capitalist living in what at that time was the city's most luxurious mansion, costing between $80,000 and $100,000. It stands in back of the Unitarian Church and is owned by that denomination. It was used for services until the present church was completed. Now the minister lives in an upper floor apartment and the rest of the house is given over to other church activities.

Glover bought the homesite from the Northern Pacific Railroad when it was considered revolutionary to go so far out. Granite for the baronial mansion came from a quarry ten miles away on the Little Spokane River. The woodwork was prepared in Minneapolis and was hand carved. The house, almost Elizabethan in style, was a conversation piece because it had three bath rooms—inside. Now it has nine and an elevator.

There are 22 rooms, a lot of little leaded windows and elaborate stairways. In the center is a two-story high drawing room with a mezzanine. One owner, Patrick Welch, used to place a Christmas tree there that took up the full height of the two floors.

After the panic of 1893 Glover was almost bankrupt. He mortgaged his home and it was sold to Frank H. Graves. It passed through several other hands, but is mostly remembered when Welch had it, for then it was the scene of a big ball and several weddings.

This is believed to be the third oldest house on the north side of the river at Spokane; it appeared on the tax rolls in 1887. It was built by a Coeur d'Alene mining man named Leary for his prospective bride. She changed her mind and married someone else after her fiancé is reported to have spent $50,000 on the property.

Leary sold the house at W. 908 Frederick Street to Robert W. Forrest, first mayor after Spokane incorporated. Forrest added the round tower so that from it he could watch the horse races at Corbin Park.

About 1896 the residence was purchased by James L. Ford, an investment dealer, who had a large family and lived there a number of years.

A later occupant was a Reverend Mr. Bass, who cut down some of the pine trees and held revival services in the yard.

The house stood empty several times. One occupant remodeled it and tore out much beautiful woodwork. The present owners, Mr. and Mrs. Charles Packard, are endeavoring to restore the place as much as possible.

Another early comer to Spokane was J. J. Browne, who arrived with his family in 1878. Their first home was a rural location with a hand pump at the sink, a woodshed, summer kitchen and barn. Baths were taken in a wooden wash tub in the kitchen.

The family moved from these accommodations into what is now known as the Strahorn house on West First Avenue next to the Cowles Museum. It was completed in 1885, but not in its present form. The grounds then included six blocks extending from Pacific Avenue to Riverside, the blocks east of the house and extending Coeur d'Alene Avenue. There was a steep path down the bluff and the children followed it in winter to skate on a pond made by an ice company. A big ice storage house stood beside the pond and the skating place was spoiled for the children as soon as the ice was thick enough for cutting.

J. J. Browne was in those days rated the wealthiest man in the state. He was president of the Browne National Bank, but it went under in the panic of 1893.

Robert F. Strahorn, who promoted the North Coast Railway (which became the Union Pacific), bought the residence in 1900 and engaged Kirtland Cutter to rebuild it. The place became Strahorn Pines, an Elizabethan half timber, the first home in the city with a hot-water heating system.

Features of the three-story dwelling were 20 rooms, a bowling alley, nine baths and ten fireplaces. Luxury fittings included brocade on some walls, Aubusson rugs, mosaic tile floors from an Italian palace, lighting fixtures with the Strahorn coat of arms, gold fixtures and American beauty satin panels in the music room.

Strahorn sold the house in 1929 on the basis of $100,000 valuation. When converted into apartments the following year some hand-decorated ceilings and wall panelings were saved. Apartments also were built in the brick stable.

Amasa B. Campbell, born in 1845, came from Ohio to Spokane in 1887 and joined John A. Finch in a partnership which existed until the former's death in 1912. Campbell was one of Spokane's mine boom millionaires but was entirely lacking in pride of purse. He married Grace M. Fox in 1890 in Youngstown, O. and it is for her this house, now a part of the Cowles Museum, is named. It was the gift of their daughter.

At the Museum, headquarters of the Eastern Washington State Historical Society, one may buy a booklet about the Campbell home, written by Margaret Bean. An effort has been made to restore the residence as much as possible to its original state, even to the extent of sending a sample of poppy wall paper to Japan to be matched. The guides point out original furnishings; others have had to be added from the same period. One of the unchanged items is a tapestry frieze in the entry.

The mansion is half of brick, topped with stucco and timber in Elizabethan style. The carriage house can be seen behind the glass passage connecting the residence and the museum. In the rear was a covered porch and Chinese fountain.

Kirtland Cutter was the architect. Among his European touches are the Delft tile fireplace in the dining room and the gold reception room with gold and onyx fireplace surmounted by a gold mirror. The walls of this room are covered with old rose moire silk panels and velvet drapes are of the same hue. From a Cleveland decorating firm Cutter obtained a set of gold furniture upholstered in old rose French damask. This room, with its embossed frieze and ceiling, has to be seen to be fully appreciated.

Some of the embellishments of the house are handsome beamed ceilings, a fireplace recessed in an arched enclosure in a hallway two stories high, a game room or den in the basement with a black oak poker table, a conservatory, sun room, butler's pantry, servants' dining room. A bell system made it possible to summon a maid from any room and a phone in the entrance hall reached the groom in the carriage house.

Spokane can claim an age of architectural flowering all its own, due to the juxtaposition of three circumstances—the city's fire of 1889, the vast amounts of quick profits being made from the Coeur d'Alene silver mines and the arrival of a talented architect, Kirtland Kelsey Cutter.

He was born in Cleveland, O. in 1860, attended the Students Art League in New York, toured Europe several years and studied in Dresden and Florence. He arrived in Spokane in 1886, where he had a banker uncle, Horace Cutter. The young man worked in the same bank with his relative a year or so until he got his bearings. Young Cutter and several other bachelors moved into a small house on Seventh Avenue, overlooking the town, and soon this dwelling was remodeled into a chalet.

The architect did not have long to wait before he fell in with an unusually favorable business situation. In the little town of about 15,000 inhabitants were a number of new-rich men eager to spend their money on ostentatious homes. When the fire cleaned out the heart of the city no time was lost in raising it again from the ashes. In 1889 Cutter had $568,000 in business on his drawing boards. His clients did not merely desire mansions; they wanted them appropriately decked out inside. Cutter was their man; he accepted commissions that sent him to Europe in pursuit of custom-made moldings, tiles, tapestries, friezes, lighting fixtures and wall paper.

When Cutter married he took over the house in which he and his friends had lived, enlarged and completely remodeled it. He lived there until he moved to California in 1923.

Unfortunately the home is scheduled to give way to a modern apartment house and was partially stripped when we saw it. Many persons regret that steps were not taken to preserve the place as a monument to the distinguished builder.

The dwelling clung to the hillside, nestling among great boulders. Some of the rocks were used on the roof, in keeping with its Swiss design. A motto above the main door was particularly fitting: "Old Age Falls, Time Changes and New Life Grows Out of the Ruins."

The dining room and hall were wainscoted in seven-foot panels of Oregon fir. The living room fireplace was faced with Moravian tiles. Ceilings were heavily timbered. Plate glass windows were surrounded by leaded work representing leaves, foliage and heart-shaped flowers. There were fresco paintings on the north and south walls. The newel post of the staircase represented a carved straw beehive standing seven feet from the floor and supported by trees. The reception hall was furnished in Indian style and had a fireplace in an alcove with an irridescent glass mosaic panel and a shelf supported by elephants. Outside around the house and easily read from the terrace was a frieze of mottos in Gothic letters painted in dull red and green.

The old Daniel Chase Corbin house at West 507 Seventh Avenue is the present Spokane Arts Center. It was built against the rock cliff in a once-secluded location. The large curved porches on three sides looked out on a splendid view. The style is a brick Georgian, very simple, but with attractive copper and opal glass hall light fixtures.

Corbin was born in New Hampshire in 1836. He reached the Coeur d'Alenes in 1886 to survey and secured a contract to build a concentrator. He realized the need of transportation and built the region's first railroad. He was engaged in many enterprises, among them irrigation and coal mining.

Mrs. Corbin and the children never lived in his Seventh Avenue home, as she became an invalid and went to Europe for her health. She died in Europe and her daughters remained abroad, marrying Englishmen—one the Earl of Orford.

Corbin lived in remote and lonely grandeur and had few social contacts. Daily he left home like clockwork in the mornings driving a fast pair of bay horses at breakneck pace. He rode in solitary dignity without his coachman.

In 1907 Corbin remarried. The new Mrs. Corbin ran for city commissioner, the unknown wife of a well known man. She was not elected.

Austin Corbin II joined his father in the Coeur d'Alenes in 1886 after being educated and living in Europe with his mother and sisters. His father was then constructing the Coeur d'Alene Railroad and Navigation Co. and he put his son in charge of the steamboat line on the lake linking the narrow gauge from Cataldo to Burke with the Northern Pacific at Hauser Junction.

Young Corbin was born in Denver, where his father had taken the family at the height of the gold excitement. While studying in Europe he met Cutter, who was also a student, and they struck up a friendship and took walking trips together. Then in 1889 they found themselves both in Spokane, where Corbin had moved to become general manager of the Spokane Falls and Northern Railroad, which his father was building. Young Corbin worked closely in all his parent's enterprises and, like his father, remained aloof from social affairs.

Austin in 1894 married the daughter of a Spokane pioneer wholesale grocer and the pattern of his life changed, for his wife and daughters liked to entertain extensively.

The 17-room Corbin home at West 815 Seventh Avenue was built in 1898 of cream brick with pillars, in colonial style, and cost $65,000. It was sur-

rounded with seven acres of grounds extending from Seventh to Ninth Avenues. The house stressed Southern decor, had many fireplaces and much hardwood trim. In keeping with its style, the Corbins engaged a Negro butler and a Negro nurse for the children.

This red brick at West 2221 First Avenue, Spokane has had two prominent owners in the past. It was erected by Jay P. Graves, who moved to Spokane in 1887 and got into real estate and investments and then into smelting and mining British Columbia copper. In 1903 he helped organize the Spokane Traction Co. and a couple of railroads which were later consolidated. He became president of the line resulting from the merger, the Spokane and Inland Empire Railroad Co.

Graves moved into his town house on First Avenue probably in the late 1890's. About 1911 he had Cutter build him another home on the Little Spokane River costing $600,000. He called it Waikiki. It had 16 rooms and a five-car garage. It sold in 1936 and was used as Gonzaga University's retreat house. All of Waikiki is now part of a realty development.

The purchaser of the town house was Aubrey Lee White, the man who made Spokane garden-conscious. He was an interesting person with an unusual combination of talents. As a financier he was successful in land business and in the financial aspects of Spokane traction. He was in railroads, irrigation and mining. He became a civic improvement leader, a member of the park board and the Chamber of Commerce. For 26 years he was head of the civic development department of the Spokesman Review and its garden editor.

While he lived on First Avenue his home was noted for hospitality. In 1920 he and his wife, Ethelyn, moved to the J. W. Binkley farm at Little Spokane, which she had inherited from her father.

Edward J. Roberts built the dwelling below at West 1923 First Avenue, Spokane about 1894. He arrived in the West with D. C. Corbin as chief engineer of construction for the Spokane Falls and Northern Railroad. Roberts had been the previous year chief engineer for the Great Northern from Minot, N.D. to Great Falls, Mont. After moving to Spokane he worked on other roads and was general manager of the Sweeney mines in Coeur d'Alene. In 1911 he was superintendent of the Spokane International Railroad and Union Iron Works.

On the grounds of his home is still to be seen a substantial carriage house.

Although the John Aylard Finch mansion at West 2304 First Avenue, Spokane, is divided into apartments, it retains much of its early charm. The entry and staircase are embellished with leaded glass in the windows, a mahogany pillar with carved garlands for newel post, mahogany railing and a long settee upholstered in red on the stair landing. Columns support an arch and the winding portion of the stair. Carved mahogany chairs and great oil paintings in heavy gold frames are exactly as they were when the Finches occupied the place. Their 18 rooms in those days included an art gallery.

The column motif appears throughout the house, in the exterior and interior, such as the delicate columns in bronze fireplace fittings. This was a Kirtland Cutter design.

Finch was an Englishman who came to the United States as a boy. He went to Spokane in 1887 and began acquiring property in the Coeur d'Alenes. He was a partner of Campbell and together they became leaders of mining in the inland empire. Finch was president of many companies. He was married in 1896 to beautiful Charlotte Swingler of Spokane and erected the house the following year.

The couple had no children, but they had a passion for spacious homes. In 1903 they had Cutter design a summer place for them at Hayden Lake with 13 bed rooms.

When Finch died he left 40 per cent of his estate to charity and civic enterprises. One of his last gifts permitted the city to develop the present arboretum.

In 1945 the remaining Finch possessions in the Spokane house were piled out under a shade tree and auctioned off. Mrs. Finch remarried and moved away to California.

The Finch Carriage House

F. Lewis Clarke, a man with a Midas touch, was described as Spokane's most eccentric millionaire. He owned one of the first automobiles in the city and used to sit in the tonneau with a brown plaid shawl over his shoulders. He employed a valet and a physical trainer.

Clarke reached Spokane in 1884 after graduating from Harvard. He invested first in a flour mill, then he made a fortune in the Coeur d'Alene and British Columbia mines. He married in 1892 and his wife, Winifred, became noted as one of the most glamorous hostesses in the city. Clarke himself gained some renown as a yachtsman, going away to participate in international sailing events.

The English-style house the couple built at West 701 Seventh Avenue in 1896 was surrounded with seven acres of grounds, including a high-walled English garden, fountain and red brick paths. The property was kept secluded by a high rock wall running 300 feet along the street. This was entered through an imposing gateway. The drive ended in a carriage house with a tall tower. There was also an ice house and a greenhouse.

In the mansion were many small windows, some arched at the top. A billiard room and a ball room were among the perquisites.

Today this home is owned by the Franciscan nuns and is part of Marycliff. Clarke erected another huge home at Hayden Lake, which later became a place to which Navy convalescents were sent.

What happens when a poor boy makes good? Usually he wants the world to know it. And what better means than sumptuous surroundings—the biggest, most elaborate house he can obtain.

The Francis-Lester at West 2208 Second Avenue, Spokane is such a place. Now a catering establishment for wedding receptions clubs and special events, it was built by Patrick Clark when he was in the money.

Clark commissioned Kirtland Cutter to build and partially furnish the Moorish mansion, the cost reportedly being around a cool million dollars. The plan called for three stories, 26 rooms and a carriage house and reportedly two years went into achieving Clark's goal.

Cutter went to Europe for the fittings. He purchased the sepia sandstone in Italy and gopher wood (mentioned in the Bible) for the regal dining room. The ends of the beams in its ceiling have 29 monks' heads looking down on the diners. Each of these faces, carved in Europe, has a different expression.

The vestibule and entry hall are of Moorish design, but the workmanship is Flemish. At the head of the central staircase stood a grandfather clock of hand-carved walnut with chimes made in London. It was imported by Tiffany's especially for Clark.

Ornate fireplaces are trimmed with onyx, marble,

mosaic and gold leaf. Other fixings were Louis XIV furniture, Turkish rugs, European light fixtures, and stained glass windows at the top of the stairs in peacock-feather motif. A French artist painted the cherubs on the ceiling of the salon, where mirrors were edged in gold leaf. The artist lay on his back on a scaffolding to complete his work.

And who were the persons who lived amid this luxury? Clark was born in Ireland in 1850 and migrated to California when he was 20. He went on to Butte and became a mine foreman, then he opened the Anaconda mine for Marcus Daly and worked as his foreman. He was there seven years and then for four years with Senator William A. Clark in his mining enterprises.

By that time Clark was ready to invest for himself. He opened the Poor Man mine in the Coeur d'Alenes in 1887 and was part owner and manager. This was when he moved to Spokane. Later he operated mines in British Columbia and became an extensive investor in mining properties from there as far south as Mexico.

In 1881 Clark married Mary Stack in Butte and they had six children. The biggest wedding remembered in Spokane's early days was that of Ella Clark to Harry Richards. The bride walked down the stairs of the great house and met the groom in front of the cream onyx fireplace in the French drawing room.

Clark died in 1915 and in 1926 Mrs. Clark sold the house to Eugene Enloe. She left in it most of the furnishings. There have been several owners since and the name Francis-Lester was acquired when it was a hotel. While it was still in that category an incendiary fire did some damage in 1962 to the attic and several upstairs bed rooms. The roof, incidentally, is of tile.

As the home was completed in 1898 before hot air heating was common, it had fireplaces in almost every room.

In contrast to the great luxury of the dwelling, the Clark family kept cows because there was no milk delivery in their day. The bovines were housed in the basement of the stable. Vehicles stored on the floor above them consisted of a landau, spider and driving cart. The family maintained two Shetland ponies along with other steeds.

Ritzville

Like many another pioneer home, this one in Ritzville grew from a smaller beginning. The kitchen wing and some of the lower floor dates from about 1890, when Dr. Frank R. Burroughs began his medical practice in the town. He remodeled and enlarged the house in 1900 and 12 years later converted his stable into a garage.

The residence when completed must have been the last word in small-town mansions. Once furnished, it remained almost unchanged in the 37 years the doctor practiced in Ritzville. When taken over and converted into a museum it contained bed room and dining room suites, lace curtains, kitchen paraphernalia, 18 rocking chairs—everything the family required. Mrs. Burroughs had lived in the house five years after her husband's death in 1925 and no other family ever owned it.

The doctor journeyed from Pennsylvania in 1888 and stopped in Ritzville supposedly for a day. He received so many calls for his services that he decided to remain, although there were only 200 inhabitants in the community. He pursued his medical practice on horseback, hiring mounts at first from a livery stable. After a cayuse bolted with him he decided it would be safer to own a horse and buggy. There were days when he drove 30 to 40 miles and during a typhoid epidemic it was said he lived in the conveyance. In anticipation of blizzards in winter he carried a great coyote-skin robe, big enough to cover himself completely.

The physician's study remains a part of the museum. There one may see his long black bag containing row after row of little bottles filled with pills and powders. He poured the latter into squares of folded paper and left them with patients.

Dr. Burroughs was at various times mayor, councilman, postmaster and president of the library board. He and his wife were extremely hospitable, entertaining often in the best country style. The doctor is said to have been like a father to the whole community.

Walla Walla County

Now an apartment house, the William Kirkman home, built not later than 1876, is a Walla Walla landmark standing at the intersection of Colville and Cherry Streets. Of rose-red brick, with narrow high windows and wide doors, it is a striking example of period architecture. It had a widow's walk railed with ornamental wrought iron, and a flag pole, now gone.

Kirkman, born in England in 1831, emigrated at 20 to Boston and then to California. He followed mining there and on the Fraser River. After various business ventures, in 1866 he took an 80-mule pack train with goods from Walla Walla to the Montana mines and on this trip became interested in a milk ranch. He returned to Walla Walla two years later and engaged in stock and meat raising with John Donley, whom he bought out in 1890 and formed the Walla Walla Dressed Meat Corp. Kirkman died three years later.

Kirkman was a director of Whitman College. This school for a time owned the house and used it as a dormitory for men. It had 14 rooms, including front and back parlors, library, dining room and a kitchen with a very large pass pantry.

The house had fireplaces, mostly of marble, in the principal rooms. The stairway inside is long and straight, with a wide railing and bronze figure with a light on the newel post. Formerly there were a capacious barn and laundry and a space for the Chinese cook to live.

The Michael B. Ward house, 228 E. Poplar Street, Walla Walla, where a reception once took place for President Rutherford B. Hayes, is now converted into lodgings. The dwelling is typical of the older period, with reversed cornices that have unusual pendant ornamentation. Beneath all of the overhangs is a beaded trim, noticeable in gables, bay windows and porch. There is said to have been a look-out platform on the roof.

The date of construction is 1886. The home was moved from its original site and turned around.

Ward was a man with money and is reputed to have financed persons making up pack trains to go to the Idaho mines. The 1870 census listed him as a farmer from Ohio, aged 51, owning property valued above average—$5,000 in real estate and $10,000 in his personal estate. Another account termed him a "capitalist" who owned 330 acres of land. He went from the East to California in 1850 and to Walla Walla County in 1861. By 1886 he was in brokerage business. He died close to the turn of the century.

Victorian cottages like this one at 526 W. Alder Street, Walla Walla went up by the hundreds toward the end of the past century. This one was built by Reinhold Funk in 1896 and is still lived in by a member of the family.

Miles Conway Moore, Washington's last territorial governor, built this mansion at 725 Bryant Street, Walla Walla in 1883. He had lived previously at Second and Rose Streets. He traded the property for a section of land three miles out of town and in the fall of 1882 bought ten acres more as a site for a new house.

"We paid $150 an acre," he wrote. "My wife wanted a place where our boys could find occupation and amusement without running on the streets. We afterward bought adjacent tracts, planted an orchard. The boys fished in the creek and swam in a pond they made on the back of the place."

The barn was erected first and the family lived in it while the house went up. Late in 1883 Dr. D. S. Baker, Moore's father-in-law, sent him to New York to a stockholders meeting of the Northern Pacific Railroad. When he returned he found the family in the new house "having trouble keeping warm, the hot-air furnace being insufficient."

Moore was born in Ohio in 1845, arrived in Walla Walla in 1863 and married Mary E. Baker ten years later. He got into the mercantile business and then into the first agricultural implement company in Eastern Washington. In 1877, when he was serving as mayor, he became associated with Dr. Baker in grain buying and stayed with it until the latter's death. He mostly dealt with wheat from the Palouse and along the Snake River, transporting it out to the Lower Columbia for shipment. In 1889 Moore was briefly governor. He was interested in the Baker and Boyer Bank, the first private bank in the state, becoming vice president and in 1898 its president.

The Moore house has much spindlework, four massive chimneys, high ceilings, moldings and long windows. Before remodeling, it was a maze of pass pantries and service rooms.

Much fancy shingle and spindle work is to be seen on the W. A. Ritz house on South Ninth Street in Walla Walla. Ritz was a prominent orchardist, who came from Iowa in 1889 after the death of his relative, Philip Ritz. The latter was a pioneer nurseryman and had been active in developing the Northern Pacific Railroad. When he died in 1889 his widow remained on the 160-acre fruit ranch a mile south of the city and managed the estate. Young Ritz married her daughter, Hattie, in 1897, so the place remained in the family.

The house was built in 1895, two years before the cousins were wedded. Ritz was socially inclined and his mansion was equipped with a ball room on the third floor.

Young Ritz was regarded as among the best and most expert fruit handlers in the county and for three years was president of the Walla Walla Fruit Fair.

Only the rounded tops of some of the windows and the recessed front door are clues to the age of Miss Dorothy Elliott's house at 314 E. Poplar Street, Walla Walla. Once inside, the picture is different, for the person responsible for the broad eaves, sleeping porches and flush bay windows made few alterations of the interior. The house once was very much like the Ward home on the same street.

Miss Elliott's residence was constructed in 1888 and faced on Birch Street. It was turned around at the time of the rebuilding in 1905. The original owner was a Mr. Small, but it was soon bought by P. C. Elliott, who was in the insurance business and later in real estate. His wife was a daughter of Dr. D. S. Baker, Walla Walla's first banker, who built the famous "strap iron" railroad to the Columbia River.

Ceilings in the house are 12 feet. There were fireplaces in the parlor, sitting room, dining room and two bed rooms. In the remodeling two of these were lost and the parlor fireplace was altered. One upstairs is of painted molded iron.

The most impressive feature is the staircase with 65 handsomely carved cherrywood banisters, a wide curved rail and ornate newel post. Pressed leather wainscoting lines the stair wall and some of the rooms. A few of the original shutters are in the house.

Miss Elliott has stored in her home quantities of early-day relics intended for a Daughters of the Pioneers museum. Among these pieces is a bed in which the first territorial governor, Isaac I. Stevens, slept.

At the corner of Rose and Tucanon Streets stands the residence of Dr. James F. Cropp, pioneer Walla Walla physician. He was born in Virginia in 1854 and journeyed west with his parents in 1872. He attended a log-cabin school, worked in hayfields in summer and taught in winter. In 1876 he worked his way to San Francisco to study medicine and later in the same manner went on to Jefferson Medical College in Philadelphia. Following graduation in 1878 he returned to Walla Walla and was married the next year. In 1890 he built the Walla Walla Hospital.

The house was erected in 1900. It has a long drawing room across the front with a fireplace in one end, and another fireplace is in the living room. Much company and gracious living are associated with the home.

The Colonial Funeral Home at the corner of Palouse and Birch Streets, Walla Walla, occupies the former residence of Frank W. Reese, dentist. It was built in 1896 in what was then the very grand manner.

Dr. Reese, member of a prominent family, was born near Walla Walla and studied dentistry at the University of Pennsylvania, graduating in 1891. He was a son of Raymond R. Reese, one of the founders of The Washington Statesman, who in 1865 abandoned journalism for the mercantile business. The father served terms as county treasurer and representative in the legislature.

The former Max Baumeister home at Stone and Edwards Streets, Walla Walla is noteworthy for its many railed porches, its porte cochere and large third-floor windows.

When built in 1900 the dwelling was just outside the city limits and stood alone on a 13-acre tract. Now it is well surrounded.

Baumeister, born in Germany in 1840, was 14 when he emigrated to the United States. He was in California before arriving in Walla Walla in 1863. He walked in from Wallula. Baumeister then understood little English, but he was hard working and he succeeded in business, going eventually into real estate, insurance and loans. He died in 1909. Mrs. Baumeister went on living in the mansion some years after his death.

H. D. G. Cox built this house in Prescott, Walla Walla County, about 1900. It was longer identified with the Joseph Utter family, who moved in around 1907.

Jonathan Pettijohn, the first settler in that part of the Touchet River Valley, in 1882 sent for Utter to teach the children in the family. Utter did this in winter and in summers he worked on a ranch of his own, five miles west of Prescott. Later Utter moved to town and operated a store. The building it occupied can be seen on the highway, a few blocks west of the house.

A member of the Utter family recalled that the Coxes were from the South and they patterned their house after one the wife has lived in as a girl. The tower room was intended as a sewing room, but Utter had a big family and one of his children slept there.

The parlor was shut off from the rest of the house with sliding doors and seldom was used except for important visitors. The dining room served as the main living room. Each room in the house had a heating stove. Small stained glass window panes were a fashionable touch in the front hall.

William Perry Bruce crossed the plains in 1850 and 11 years later arrived in the Touchet Valley, searching for a location where his wife's health might improve. He bought a homestead claim at the confluence of Coppei Creek and Touchet River in 1862 and moved his family into a log cabin on the rise of ground where Main and West Third Streets, Waitsburg intersect. A deep spring was at the foot of the hill behind the cabin and here the Bruces' two-year-old son toddled down and drowned.

In 1864 a water-powered flour mill was started by Sylvester Wait and the village of Waitsburg began. Bruce contributed land and money toward starting the mill but made no effort to lay out a townsite on his property until five years later.

He was prominent in the growth of Waitsburg, helped found a Republican newspaper, was a merchant, farmer and county commissioner. His nine-room house, built at Main and West Third Streets in 1883, became a center of activities and the spacious yard was the scene of ice cream socials.

Bruce died in 1888 and his wife went on living in the residence another three years.

Mrs. Mary E. Weller bought the house in 1922 from the Bruce heirs and planned it for a public library. Because of extensive repairs needed and the cost of upkeep, the town refused the gift. For nine years it was unoccupied and suffered considerable damage. Then, in 1931, after her mother's death, Fanny E. Weller decided to carry out the plan and conducted a small library there. Since the building had no lights, it was open only for limited periods. Management problems became too difficult and ultimately the project had to be given up and the house was again locked. Its windows have been boarded to protect it from vandalism and there is a question as to what use can be made of it. A movement has several times been on foot to convert it into a museum.

This is remembered as the Ed Baxter house at 200 W. Fourth Street, Waitsburg, though it had an earlier, now-forgotten owner. It dates from the first years of the 1880's. The Baxters once ran a boarding house there, but now the place is remodelled into apartments.

In 1909 A. M. McCoy erected his home at 331 Coppei Avenue, Waitsburg. He had a lumber yard behind his house and his wife kept the books for him in one of the rooms of the home. Later a small house was built in back to serve as office.

The first Mrs. McCoy died and the second Mrs. McCoy was instrumental in building an addition on the rear, to allow more space for entertaining.

The room upstairs with the angled roof is the master's bed room. At the right, where the small windows are, is a dressing alcove.

This house was noted for the hospitality of its occupants. It was quaint and pretty inside and had an attractive little dining room at the left end of the porch with ornamental glass in it. The house was well built and considered one of the finest in town.

The stump in front is all that remains of a huge maple which shaded the place.

Dayton

Dayton has approximately 75 Nineteenth Century houses still occupied. It was a community that remained settled after the flurry of being a jumping-off place for the Orofino gold mines was over. As in Walla Walla, the railroad company boosted the sale of land. The town is in a fertile belt, where crop failures are almost unknown.

The old Robinett house at 1203 S. Fourth Street is not in as good shape as some of the others, nevertheless it is worthy of notice for its overhanging roof lines and its window frames, particularly the small arched one upstairs in front.

Robinett and his partner, Rainwater, were saw-mill men who both built homes on South Fourth Street before 1878. A mountain was named for the Robinett family.

John Brinning, a native of Austria, built this house at 410 First Avenue, Dayton before 1884. He had moved to the town in 1877.

The remarkable feature of this residence is the mosaic glass trim at the top of the front gable. The house has much spindlework and a square-pat-terned molding which extends over the porches. The original shutters are in place. J. A. Boldman owned the house for 30 years.

Like most of Dayton's venerable homes, it has been kept in excellent repair.

This is the old Carr house at Third and Fremont Streets in Dayton. Carr was a builder, who picked out his lumber carefully. The interior was beautifully finished and the exterior embellished with spindlework, fancy shingles and knobby festoons over some of the windows. Two types of fans or sunbursts were used in small gables.

There are two fireplaces, much colored glass and a double front door. This is a side view of the residence, which stands on a corner lot.

This house at Fourth and Oak Streets, Dayton is of brick from the old Dexter brickyard. It is one of several that Dexter built in the same period, moving around to the next as he sold them. The arches on this home are eye-catching.

To residents of Dayton this is known as the house with the footbridge, for it is fronted with a slender span across a depression where a creek flows only part of the time. The dwelling was built in 1878 by an attorney named Higgins and was owned for many years by the Gillis-Richardson family. Mrs. Gillis-Richardson was the only woman in town who had a chauffeur.

Present owners are the Zastrows.

There is a resemblance between this and the Brinning home; both have the square-patterned molding over the porch, indicating they must have been built about the same time. A fan design is over the front entrance.

Some remodeling was done in recent years, the owners removing several interior walls and putting the two parlors and front hall together in order to create a spacious room.

"I held my breath when the contractor removed the braces," Mrs. Zastrow said, "but the beams overhead were solid and nothing happened."

At Washington Avenue and Second Street, Dayton is the C. J. Broughton home, which has been maintained since the death of Mrs. Broughton in 1963 for use by members of the family. It is still in excellent condition and remains unchanged inside and out.

It was built about 1885 by M. A. Baker, who was in real estate and investments. In 1892 Broughton, pioneer banker, merchant and farmer, purchased it. His wife always said he married her in one end of town and walked her to the other end to her new home and that was her honeymoon. Her nine children were born in the gracious mansion.

At the time of their marriage Broughton was operating a store. He made a fortune in Dayton and his widow, who lived to 96, was one of the wealthiest women in the county.

The house has 12 foot ceilings, a front and a back parlor and a downstairs bed room.

Nothing has been moved in the way of furniture and the place is filled with wonderful antiques. One interesting piece is a kitchen treasure—a table with bins and overhead storage space—made long ago by a Dayton furniture factory.

Like the station at Fairfield, the one at Dayton was meant to be lived in. The stationmaster's family could enjoy a three-way walk-around porch and a bay window facing the tracks. The bargeboards along the roof offered an unusual style of ornamentation and the trim on the end windows was designed to match them.

Dayton acquired its first tracks in July, 1881, when the first Oregon Railway and Navigation Co. passenger train ran in from Walla Walla. The depot was not erected on its present site, but on Cameron Street in Railroad Addition, near Rock Hill. A hotel, the Cameron House, was built across the street from it.

When a second railroad, the Hunt Line, reached Dayton in 1889 (it later became the Northern Pacific) the station was moved to its present location, though the rival company built another just opposite it. Both are still in use, the older now serving the Union Pacific.

For many years this building was conspicuous for its bright paint and the gay flower garden which the stationmaster maintained behind the freight shed.

217

Klickitat County

Charles Newell erected Goldendale's "red house" in 1890. He owned land north of the present Pleasant Valley grange hall and bought horses from the Indians, selling the animals in Chicago. Since he did not want to leave his beauteous wife alone in the valley while he was away on trips east, he built the chalet in town, following her wishes in designing it. The color was chosen because of her fondness for bright hues.

Mrs. Newell was one quarter Indian and three quarters French. She loved fine clothes and Newell brought her wearing apparel from Chicago. Despite her fashionable furbelows, the ladies of the community did not accept her socially.

Finally the couple left Goldendale for Toppenish, where Newell built and operated a hotel.

The 10-room house is presently owned by Franklin Miller and has undergone some interior remodeling. However, its stained-glass window panes, imported from Europe, and the Gothic trim are just as they were nearly 80 years ago.

Goldendale's Historical Museum was long the home of Winthrop B. Presby, an attorney. It is noteworthy for the ironwork on the rooftop, round cupalos, decor of the entrance hall and circular stairway. It has four fireplaces, three of them to one chimney.

The house was erected in 1902, one of the 13 rooms serving Mr. Presby as his office. Some family furnishings remain, including a marble-topped cherrywood buffet with shelves. Other articles on loan date back as far as the days of John Golden and his bride, who arrived with six other families in 1859 and founded the town.

Maryhill, on the Columbia River in Klickitat County, was intended as a home but never was completed as such. The builder was Sam Hill, son-in-law of James J. Hill, the railroad magnate. The former arrived in Seattle in the 1890's and at first was interested in buying up Okanogan County farm land. He was discouraged from there by a plague of locusts and in 1905 began purchasing property on the Columbia until at length he had 6,700 acres running for five miles along the river.

After much consultation with scientists and meteorological experts he selected a site for an Italian castle in which to reside. He chose a place at what was then the rural orchard community of Columbus and changed its name to Maryhill in honor of his wife and daughter. He said it was the garden spot of the world, where the warm winds of spring first struck.

The few residents of the surrounding country scratched their heads in amazement when they saw Hill's dream taking shape in 1914. The Grecian Doric building was three stories high, had 40 rooms and concrete walls 42 inches thick. A New York architect designed the castle, which was slightingly referred to as "Sam Hill's Folly." The big banquet hall on the ground floor was to be one of the great rooms of American houses. At either end was a huge fireplace. Heavy bronze gratings were at doors and windows to protect the jewels of expected guests. The royal coat of arms of Belgium was carved in stone over the main entrance and ramps were provided over which the carriages of royal guests were to be driven to and from the principal door.

It is understood that Hill expected to entertain King Albert of Belgium, among other distinguished persons.

Construction was interrupted by the First World War and was not resumed until the 1920's. The house was a skeleton for 14 years, the habitat of rats and swallows.

During the war Hill had been active in Rumania's behalf and he succeeded in persuading Queen Marie to journey to Maryhill in November, 1926 and dedicate the great mansion as an international museum of fine arts, since by then he had given up the intention of living in it. Princess Ileana, who accompanied her mother, remembered it as "the wildest and most desolate spot she had ever seen."

In May, 1940, nine years after Hill's death, the place finally was opened as a museum. The builder had left funds for carrying out his wishes. Queen Marie donated many items to the displays and called Hill a great builder and a dreamer.

He was a good roads booster and constructed the first paved road in Washington at Maryhill. It was less than a mile long.

WHAT BECOMES OF OLD HOUSES?

"Okanogan" Smith cabin as it was. Courtesy Okanogan County Historical Society.

Some old houses are allowed to decay until they are an eyesore and fire or a wrecker is permitted to finish them off.

Some, beloved by a family, are kept in good repair and, when no one remains alive to cherish them, the more fortunate are snapped up by the owner of antiques, who finds them just the place for displaying collector's treasures. In these days of scanty wall space an old house can be a boon to the possessor of prints and paintings, tapestries and shadow boxes. With a modernized kitchen and some attention to heating and lighting arrangements such a home offers many compensations.

Mansions of the wealthy generally have been converted into apartments. It is surprising how much desirable storage space can be found in such suites. No one can take adequate care of huge homes any more; younger members of families do not want them since the day of retinues of maids and gardeners is past.

A more melancholy employment for some of these spacious homes has been conversion into funeral parlors. The large rooms are just what the undertaker wants and, as a consequence, numerous venerable dwellings that once were thronged with social groups now are smartly painted, brilliantly illuminated burial establishments.

A few others have served as college dormitories or clubs. A recent use has been as homes for alcoholics and parolees. Some have been considered for museums in small communities.

If old houses could be arbiters of their fate probably the most rewarded would be those whose owners cherish old glass, restore fireplaces or delight in searching out cherrywood railings, pieces of scrollwork and paneled doors to replace modern substitutions. Many period houses in Washington now are in better shape than ever in their past, furnished in excellent taste and with more comfort than their original owners enjoyed.

INDEX

DATE DUE

MAY 26 1999	